TOP CHEFS

EMERIL LAGASSE

LAKE PARK HIGH SCHOOL
ROSELLE, IL 60172

TOP CHEFS

OTHER TITLES IN THIS SERIES:

EMERIL LAGASSE

SAWYER ALBRIGHT

Produced by OTTN Publishing, Stockton, New Jersey.

Eldorado Ink
PO Box 100097
Pittsburgh, PA 15233
www.eldoradoink.com

CPSIA compliance information: Batch#TC010112-4. For further
information, contact Eldorado Ink at info@eldoradoink.com.

First printing

1 3 5 7 9 8 6 4 2

Library of Congress Cataloging-in-Publication Data

Albright, Sawyer.
  Emeril Lagasse / Sawyer Albright.
    p. cm. — (Top chefs)
  Includes bibliographical references and index.
  ISBN 978-1-61900-016-2 (hc)
  ISBN 978-1-61900-017-9 (pb)
  ISBN 978-1-61900-018-6 (ebook)
  1. Lagasse, Emeril—Juvenile literature. 2. Celebrity chefs—United
States—Biography—Juvenile literature. I. Title.
  TX649.L34A43 2012
  641.5092—dc23
  [B]
                              2011052791

For information about custom editions, special sales, or
premiums, please contact our special sales department at
info@eldoradoink.com.

TABLE OF CONTENTS

New Orleans chef Emeril Lagasse has combined cooking skill with an exuberant personality to become one of today's most famous celebrity chefs.

CHAPTER ONE

"WE'RE COMING BACK"

Emeril Lagasse loves food, especially the dishes of his adopted hometown of New Orleans, Louisiana. Through his television programs and books, the charismatic chef has inspired millions of people to enjoy food and cooking. When he first appeared on national television in the 1990s, Lagasse presented a new image of the gourmet chef. Lagasse was no cold, disdainful perfectionist. He was a hardworking regular guy who happened to be passionate about food and about making people happy.

In 2005 the culinary director of Lagasse's restaurants, Dave McCelvey, said of the celebrity chef, "There's no smoke and mirrors. He doesn't put on an act. He really is gregarious and charismatic and caring. And people just flip over him."

But that year there were some people who questioned how caring Lagasse was when he was forced to handle one of the most difficult times of his career. In August 2005 his close ties with New Orleans, the home of three of his award-winning restaurants, were tested, when one of the worst natural catastrophes ever to hit the United States struck the central Gulf coast.

HURRICANE KATRINA

On August 29, 2005, New Orleans was hit by an extremely powerful hurricane. The storm, named Katrina, had moved across the Gulf of Mexico, intensifying in size and force as it absorbed energy from the gulf's warm waters. At one point Hurricane Katrina was classified as a category 5 storm, the most powerful type of hurricane, with sustained winds of more than 160 miles per hour. By the time Katrina made landfall in southeastern Louisiana, the storm designation had fallen to category 3, with an average wind speed of around 125 miles per hour.

Still, the damage was severe. The hurricane's high winds downed trees and power lines carrying electricity to homes and businesses. Heavy rainfall, more than an inch per hour, pelted a great swath of the region. Ultimately 8 to 10 inches of rain fell along Katrina's path. Rivers and streams overflowed, flooding streets, homes, and stores. Flooding also

(Left) Satellite image of Hurricane Katrina making landfall in Louisiana and Mississippi early on the morning of August 29, 2005. The powerful storm caused extensive flooding in New Orleans (opposite).

As the flood waters receded, scenes of incredible devastation were uncovered. The damage was so extensive that many people believed New Orleans would never recover from Hurricane Katrina.

resulted from the storm surge, a rise in sea level along the coast caused by the hurricane's strong winds.

Katrina devastated many areas along the central Gulf coast, causing the most extensive damage in the states of Alabama, Mississippi, and Louisiana. More than 1,700 lives were lost, and approximately 275,000 homes were destroyed. Hundreds of thousands of people were displaced, forced to leave the region in search of food and shelter.

A FLOODED CITY

New Orleans sits six feet below sea level, and is surrounded by water. Lake Pontchartrain lies to the north, and the city straddles the Mississippi River as it starts to empty into the nearby Gulf of Mexico. Under normal conditions, New Orleans is kept dry by a system of levees designed to prevent flooding.

When Hurricane Katrina struck, the heavy rainfall and 22-foot-high storm surge caused the levees separating the city from Lake Pontchartrain to fail in three places. Within two days almost 80 percent of New Orleans was under water. Those residents who had been able to evacuate before the hurricane hit stayed away as the magnitude of the disaster became apparent. The city was shut down, as state and federal agencies worked to rescue those trapped by the flooding, and to provide food, shelter, and clean water to those left homeless by the disaster.

Businesses in the New Orleans area had suffered billions of dollars in damage, and the owners had to figure out what they would do next. Before the storm, New Orleans had been one of America's most popular tourist destinations. But with the extent of the damage to the city, it was clear that the tourism industry would be crippled for a year or more. This would make it hard for businesses that depended on tourists, such as restaurants and hotels, to survive. A week after the storm hit, the *New York Times* quoted one New Orleans restaurant owner who said he planned to permanently relocate his business, because "there's not going to be tourism for many years."

EMERIL'S RESTAURANTS

Like other restaurant owners in New Orleans, Emeril Lagasse faced an uncertain future. The storm shut down his three restaurants in the city—Emeril's, in the Warehouse District; NOLA Restaurant, in the French Quarter; and Emeril's Delmonico, in the Garden District. His New Orleans corporate headquarters, known as Emeril's Homebase, also suffered damage from the storm and subsequent flooding.

Emeril's Homebase and his restaurants employed hundreds of people, and Lagasse's first concern was to see what had happened to them. He temporarily relocated the corporate business operations to Atlanta and eventually determined that all company employees had survived.

On September 16, 2005, Emeril released a statement in which he said he would work to help bring the city back. "Over the past two weeks, I have focused on making sure my family, my friends, and my staff are safe," he said. "The city

In 2005 many people considered New Orleans to be one of the most important food and beverage capitals of the nation. More than 10 percent of the New Orleans workforce—about 55,000 people—had jobs in the city's 3,400 restaurants.

of New Orleans is my home and it is a place that I love and my heart goes out to the many victims of the hurricane. I am completely dedicated to rebuilding this great city."

Emeril expressed his concern for his employees and families who had been displaced by the hurricane and noted that his company was working to find jobs for them in cities where he had restaurants. He also insisted that he would reopen his three restaurants in New Orleans as soon as possible. "The New Orleans restaurant industry has an unbelievable spirit—and we're all dedicated and passionate about our cuisine, and our community," he said. "I have no doubt that it will be a struggle, but I look forward to building a new New Orleans and an even better food city in the future."

CONTROVERSY

But Emeril did not immediately return to New Orleans. That October he went ahead with a previously scheduled publicity tour for his latest cookbook. The tour took him to cities across the country—everywhere but New Orleans.

In mid-October, restaurant writer Brett Anderson of the *Times-Picayune* noted that Emeril's three New Orleans restaurants were still closed and that Homebase employees had been laid off. His article, entitled "Where's Emeril?," complained that the chef's face appeared that month on the cover of magazines like *Gourmet* and *Cigar Aficionado*, but that Lagasse himself had not been seen at all in the beleaguered city.

Emeril was quoted in Anderson's article as saying, "I know this is a major catastrophe, but I work so far in advance. My things are planned, my people are planned." Even though he wasn't in the city, Emeril insisted, "I don't know anyone out there who's been more rah-rah for the city of New Orleans in the last couple of weeks."

"DOING WHAT I CAN DO"

Emeril Lagasse and his team were working behind the scenes. They contributed to fundraisers and benefits to help victims of Katrina. They worked to find jobs in the food industry for refugees. And they worked to ensure that Emeril's restaurants reopened as quickly as possible.

Two months after the storm, on November 2, 2005, Emeril's office released a statement announcing that the New Orleans corporate office, Emeril's Homebase, was back in business in the city. The press release also said that Emeril's and NOLA would reopen in December. Lagasse expressed his pleasure at making this announcement. "We are very happy to reopen our doors, reuniting with our friends, and all of our loyal customers through the years," he said. "I love this city, and I look forward to working together to build an even better New Orleans in the future." But no reopening date was indicated for Emeril's Delmonico, Emeril's third restaurant in the city.

On December 8, 2005, four months after Katrina spun through Louisiana, Emeril's was open again. NOLA opened a week later. Getting back to the business of running and serving customers his special cuisines was important to Emeril. In January 2006 he told the *Naples Daily News*, "It's sad a city could be so devastated. I'm there. I'm giving it my all trying to do what I can do."

Due to extensive damage, Emeril's Delmonico would remain closed for more than a year, not opening its doors until October 2006. That month Lagasse told the *Dallas Morning News* that it was still difficult to find workers and places for them to live in New Orleans. "Staffing and housing have been the problems," Emeril said. "But to me, it's important to make people smile. I've poured my heart and soul into

FUNDRAISING AFTER HURRICANE KATRINA

In the weeks after Katrina struck, Emeril Lagasse and his company contributed to and set up fundraising events to help people whose lives were devastated by the hurricane. One was a benefit concert called Miami Rocks for Relief that featured Gloria Estefan and Queen Latifah, held September 30, 2005. Before the concert Lagasse, along with celebrity chef Norman Van Aken, cohosted a fundraising dinner. Among the recipients of the money raised were the Emeril Lagasse Employee Disaster Relief Fund, MusiCares Hurricane Relief Fund, and the American Red Cross.

Another event took place on October 2, 2005, in Atlanta, Georgia. At Crescent City ThrowDown, diners listened to Louisiana music and ate food prepared by the chef de cuisine of Emeril's, Chris Wilson. Funds went to assist New Orleans-based musicians and those who worked in the music industry.

Lagasse also helped raise funds through his charitable organization, the Emeril Lagasse Foundation. It held a fundraising gala, called the Carnivale du Vin, on October 29, 2005, at the Venetian Resort Hotel and Casino in Las Vegas. In publicizing the event, Lagasse noted, "Carnivale du Vin will pay tribute to New Orleans, celebrating the spirit and undeniable energy of the city, while helping raise funds for children in New Orleans whose lives have been affected by Katrina." The benefit raised $1.4 million.

Gloria Estefan and Emeril Lagasse arrive at the Miami Rocks for Relief benefit, September 2005.

New Orleans, night and days, these last months. It's home. And slowly, we're coming back."

RESTAURATEUR OF THE YEAR

As the extent of Emeril's work during the long slow recovery became clear, the celebrity chef drew praise from the media. In January 2007 *New Orleans CityBusiness* restaurant critic Tom Fitzmorris named Emeril Lagasse "Restaurateur of the Year." Fitzmorris noted that Lagasse had reopened his restaurants at a time when few tourists were venturing into New Orleans. "His restaurants Emeril's and NOLA relied to a large extent on visitor business, which did not reappear in significant numbers until a year later." And he pointed out that Lagasse continued to support the city by holding and contributing to numerous fundraisers. For all his efforts in New Orleans, Emeril deserved praise. "In the aftermath of the storm," Fitzmorris concluded, "Emeril was a hero."

Years later, in an interview with the *New York Times*, Lagasse would discuss the early criticism that he received. "They were taking potshots at me because I wasn't wearing waders and crying in front of the restaurant," he said. "But I was being a businessman, working on saving the business."

Lagasse's efforts and those of thousands of others who worked to rebuild the city succeeded in bringing New Orleans' tourism industry back. By May 2008, the New Orleans Tourism Marketing Corporation was able to report that the number of tourists had rebounded to pre-Katrina figures. The businessman celebrity chef had stood by his adopted hometown and helped New Orleans to make a remarkable comeback from the devastating storm.

CHAPTER TWO

BOY IN AN APRON

The celebrity chef who today is identified with New Orleans began life far away from that southern city, in a Massachusetts town called Fall River. But like the multicultural city of New Orleans, Fall River—located in the southeastern part of Massachusetts—was also a home for immigrants from many different countries.

FALL RIVER, MASSACHUSETTS

The name "Fall River" comes from the Pokanoket Wampanoag Indian tribe that inhabited the area in the 1600s. They called the local river "Quequechan," which is believed to mean "Leaping or Falling Waters." Food was plentiful in the region, which had an abundance of game and fish.

With its access to Mount Hope Bay on the Taunton River and the plentiful waterpower of the Quequechan River, the area soon attracted colonial settlers. By the early 1700s some of them were harnessing the power of the Quequechan waterfalls to run sawmills, gristmills (for grinding grain), and iron works. In the early 1800s the town of Fall River was founded, and its population quickly grew as textile companies established mills along the river. By the late 1800s there were more than 100 mills, and Fall River had become the leading cotton textile-manufacturing center in the United States.

The town also became a center for European immigrants in search of jobs as mill workers. By 1900 Fall River was home to around 26,000 textile workers. Most came from the countries of Ireland, Poland, France, and Portugal. They lived in inexpensive mill housing, typically forming close-knit communities of people from the same families or villages of the "old country."

Today these ethnic neighborhoods remain an important feature of Fall River. The city's largest ethnic group is Portuguese, with the 2008 U.S. Census indicating that 48.6 percent of the city residents are of Portuguese descent. About 6 percent are French Canadian. Emeril Lagasse claims heritage to both those groups.

PORTUGUESE ALL THE WAY

John Emeril Lagasse III was born on October 15, 1959, to Hilda Medeiros Lagasse, who is Portuguese American, and Emeril Lagasse Jr., who is French Canadian. Emeril was the middle child of the couple's three kids. He grew up with an older sister, Delores, and a younger brother, Mark. Hilda and Mr. John, as Emeril's father was known, had grown up and gone to school together in Fall River. Married since 1950, they lived with their children in a wood-frame house in the Maplewood section of the city.

Although Fall River's textile industry had declined by the second half of the 20th century, some textile mills were still active. Emeril's father worked in a textile-finishing plant,

A view of downtown Fall River in the early 1920s, as the small Massachusetts city appeared when Emeril's parents were growing up there.

Duro Finishing, where he spent his days dyeing suit linings. To make extra money, John Lagasse also worked as a cab-driver and as a security guard. Hilda was a stay-at-home mom who took care of the house and children.

Emeril grew up speaking Portuguese, attending the Portuguese parish of Santo Christo Church, and living in a Portuguese community. He also ate a lot of Portuguese food, much of it cooked by Hilda. He would later say that he was raised "Portuguese all the way."

Emeril credits his mother for his love of food. Hilda, he says, was a good cook, who enjoyed preparing meals for the family. Much of the Lagasse family life revolved around the

The Portuguese identity in Fall River is not as strong as it used to be, a local newspaper warned in 2010. It reported that many Portuguese families had moved to the suburbs and that since 1980 the number of immigrants coming to the city from Portugal and the Azores had declined significantly.

kitchen and family members typically ate and cooked together. Emeril has said that food from both his mother's and father's cultures were an important part of growing up, pointing out, "We always had the value of the family table and these cultural influences."

MUSIC AND COOKING

Emeril was just four years old when he demonstrated a gift for music, revealing an ability to play several instruments. He mastered the drums, and at age eight was the percussionist for the local 45-member Portuguese band. The group toured on weekends in the summer to places as far away as Canada.

Emeril also showed an intense interest in cooking when he was young. He often watched his mother as she prepared the ingredients, washed and chopped vegetables, or seasoned a roast before putting it in the oven. When he was too small to reach the counter and stove, he stood on a wooden stool so he could see what Hilda was doing. As he grew older, he insisted on helping.

One of Hilda's memories is of her seven-year-old son helping put vegetables in a soup pot. "He wanted to be right there, put the vegetables in. But I would show him how to do it, slowly with a spoon. But sometimes, believe me, he used to get in my way, right in my way. He was always in front of the stove."

Hilda taught her son many cooking techniques and Portuguese recipes. "The first thing that I cooked was a vegetable soup with my mom," Emeril would later recall. "I guess I was eight or nine years old. I came home from school and worked at the stove with her and I can remember working at it for a long time until I finally got this soup perfected, that we could serve it to the family."

Another kitchen where young Emeril was welcome was that of Ines de Costa, who ran a restaurant in nearby Swansea. The Lagasse family would often visit the restaurant, and young Emeril would venture into Ines's kitchen. There, she showed him how to make Portuguese food specialties like chouriço (a spicy smoked sausage) and stuffed quahogs (better known as hard-shell clams). No cooking lesson would have been complete without learning how to make a hearty Portuguese soup—broth transformed by adding kale and cabbage, beans and beef, some ground chorizo, and salt.

BAKERY JOB

As a boy, Emeril helped out around the house. One of his after-school chores was to walk to the neighborhood Portuguese bakery to buy bread for dinner. He enjoyed his visits to the Moonlight Bakery. "I'd walk in and there was just

Emeril has said he grew up watching the cooking shows of Julia Child. Her first television series, *The French Chef*, originally ran from 1963 to 1973.

something about it, these smells and aromas, and I was just intrigued by it," Lagasse recalled later in an interview. Soon, he asked for a job.

Emeril was 10 years old when he began working at the Moonlight Bakery. He was given the job of washing pots and pans in the kitchen. He made one dollar an hour and worked for four hours each day after school. By age 12 Emeril had

INES DE COSTA

Born in São Miguel, Azores (an autonomous region of Portugal), the chef credited with helping Emeril learn how to cook came to the United States in 1952 at the age of 19. Ines married her husband, Manuel De Costa, two year later. After operating restaurants in New York and Vermont, the two opened an eatery in Swansea, Massachusetts, about five miles northeast of Fall River.

In 1978, with plans to retire from the restaurant business, Ines sold the Swansea eatery, but three weeks later she began running the restaurant at St. John's Athletic Club in Fall River, located near John and Hilda Lagasse's Baker Street home. She became a fixture in the community, where people called her Vo, the Portuguese word for grandmother. "Her life was food," her daughter Ines Bates said. "Her dining room in her home was too small to feed all of her family and friends, so that restaurant became her dining room. It let her do what she loved, which was to feed and nourish people."

One of those people was Emeril, who would stop by to see Vo whenever he visited his hometown. He called De Costa his "second Mom," mentioned her often on his TV cooking shows, and credited her in some of his recipes. She even made a guest appearance on his show. De Costa continued working at St. John's until the day before her death on September 24, 2011.

worked his way up to baking breads, cakes, muffins, and sweetbreads. He later moved on to baking Portuguese specialties such as cornmeal breads and desserts like pastries and custards. "I didn't have to work," he said. "I worked because I loved it."

A love of food and cooking was a somewhat unusual hobby for a boy. During the early 1970s in Fall River, it was unheard of for men to cook or spend time in a kitchen. "[N]obody in the early '70s—especially a guy—ever cooked," Emeril would later say. "Especially where I came from." But if his friends wondered why Emeril liked to cook, he made it clear that he had interests in other things as well. He played sports and worked as a paperboy. "Hey, it's Fall River, man," he said in an interview. "I had to, like, prove I was a tough guy who just liked lookin' in the pots and pans to see what was goin' on."

High School

By the time he was a teenager, Emeril knew he was serious about cooking. So when it came time to enter high school, he chose to enroll at the Diman Regional Vocational Technical High School, which offered work-related training in the culinary arts. The school was located on Bedford Street, about a mile east of Moonlight Bakery.

While in high school Emeril worked the bakery's night shift, which ran from eleven o'clock at night until seven the next morning. After his shift ended, he went home, changed his clothes, and went to classes. He would get home from school around three o'clock in the afternoon and go to sleep until it was time to get up and go to back to work at the bakery.

This first job taught Emeril more than just the basics of baking. He also learned a great deal about people. "I remember sitting on stainless steel flour bins," he recalled. "Mom would have sent over my dinner with my dad, and when the Portuguese men would take their dinner break, I'd heat my supper in a brick oven. They took a liking to me and they'd teach me about the bread and the Portuguese specialties. If you understand people and understand their culture, then you can easily understand their food."

Despite his challenging schedule, Emeril did well in school. According to his teachers at Diman, he was an exceptional student who came to class well prepared and full of enthusiasm.

Emeril also found time in his schedule to devote to music, which was still a big part of his life. In addition to mastering the drums, he could play several other musical instruments, including the trombone, trumpet, tuba, and French horn. But he considered himself a "percussion major." Emeril played drums in the high school band. He also wrote music for several bands he was in, including the Saint Anthony Band (a Portuguese band that played orchestra music) and a local band called the Royal Aces that performed at weddings and dances. While in high school he participated in two summer camps operated by the prestigious New England Conservatory of Music.

Emeril Lagasse's senior portrait. He graduated from Diman Vocational High School in the spring of 1977.

Emeril also continued to gain experience working with food. He took a job with an upscale restaurant, where he was given the

Emeril is in the center of this photo of members of his high school band. Although he was a talented musician, he decided to make a career in cooking, not music.

opportunity to work the pantry station and in the kitchen. That was followed by a second restaurant job, where he began to realize that he liked the idea of becoming a chef more than any other option for his future.

CHOOSING COOKING

Emeril's talents as a musician earned him the offer of a full college scholarship to the New England Conservatory of Music. But the aspiring chef decided that a professional music career was not in his future. He turned down the scholarship so he could pursue a career in the culinary arts.

The decision to reject a scholarship upset Emeril's parents, particularly his mother. Hilda was appalled. "My mom freaked out," Emeril said. "I think I might have gotten chased around the neighborhood a few times. She just never thought that the cooking thing would stick."

It would take Hilda a couple of years before she recognized that the decision was right for her son. Emeril's father, on the other hand, was able to accept the idea much earlier. A day after Emeril made the announcement to his parents, his father told him in private, "[I]f you think that this is something you love, which obviously you do, and you think this is a way you can get a ticket out of here, then you go for it."

In the spring of 1977, Emeril graduated from Diman Regional Vocational Technical High School. His next stop was Johnson and Wales University in Providence, Rhode Island, about 25 miles away from his family's home. While most of Emeril's friends would stay in Fall River and work in the mills, Emeril Lagasse had a different future in mind.

CHAPTER THREE

PREP COOK TO EXEC CHEF

Making a choice between a career in music and one in the culinary arts was difficult, Emeril has said, but he knew he needed to follow his passion. Going to culinary school rather than accepting the music scholarship meant he would have to pay his way through school. But it was a choice he believed was right for him. Many years later, he would comment in an interview, "Music still is a part of my life. It's always in my head. It's just that my absolute passion and love and drive and desire is all related to food."

JOHNSON AND WALES UNIVERSITY

Lagasse enrolled in 1977 at Johnson and Wales University (JWU). Founded as a business school in Providence in 1914, the university is a nonprofit private institution. It was chartered as a junior college in 1963 by the state of Rhode Island, rechartered in 1970 as a four-year college granting baccalaureate degrees, and rechartered in 1980 to offer postgraduate degrees. The school was officially designated a university in 1988. Its emphasis is on career education, with degrees

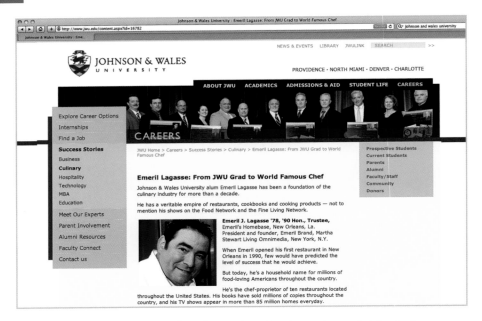

The website for Johnson and Wales University (www.jwu.edu) includes a page on Emeril Lagasse, one of the school's most famous graduates. The site notes Emeril has funded millions of dollars worth of scholarships at the school, raising the money with an annual golf tournament.

offered in business, hospitality, the culinary arts, technology, and education. Today JWU has campuses in Providence; North Miami, Florida (1992); Denver, Colorado (2000); and Charlotte, North Carolina (2004).

When Emeril enrolled at the Providence campus in 1977 the culinary program was fairly new. The associate degree program in the culinary arts had been added just a few years earlier, in 1973. Additional two- and four-year degree programs in hospitality and food service would be added later. Ultimately, Johnson and Wales would offer both two- and four-year programs in culinary arts, pastry arts, food service management, and in the hospitality fields. Today, the school is considered one of the top-ranked culinary and hospitality colleges in the world.

A Business Education

A major component of programs at JWU is exposing students to business management as well as the art of cooking. Emeril chose the school, he has said, because he was interested in learning the business side of food service. He told an interviewer, "I chose Johnson and Wales because I wanted to know more about business than about cooking. I had already been cooking for eight or nine years."

At the time he entered the school, Emeril was working at the Venus de Milo restaurant in Swansea, which was not far from the university and even closer to home. He had started there as a prep cook, tasked with peeling onions and potatoes. But he worked his way up and when he began at the university he was making good money as a chef de cuisine. The restaurant job helped pay his Johnson and Wales tuition.

At the Venus de Milo restaurant, Lagasse met fellow university student Elizabeth Kief. The two dated throughout their time in school. Emeril completed his course work for the culinary program in May 1978, and he and Elizabeth married the following October.

Job Search

His first job after graduation took Emeril to Philadelphia. He and Elizabeth moved to the city, where he worked for a time in the kitchen at the Sheraton Hotel downtown. After recognizing

Johnson and Wales awarded Emeril Lagasse an honorary doctorate degree in 1990. He has also served as a trustee at the school.

that the job was not what he wanted, Emeril decided to move to New York City.

During the late 1970s, the city of New York was considered a major culinary center of the United States. When Elizabeth and Emeril moved there, the city boasted more than 3,000 restaurants just in the borough of Manhattan.

However, in his search for better opportunities Lagasse hit a roadblock. He was American and had been trained in a U.S. culinary school. During the 1970s and early 1980s, most high-end restaurants in New York were run by French, German, or Swiss chefs who had trained in Europe. They looked down on American chefs, who were thought to know nothing about fine dining or how to prepare specialty dishes. Lagasse explained, "Americans weren't supposed to know anything about food; all we supposedly knew was about hamburgers and cheeseburgers and macaroni and cheese."

Emeril applied for jobs in the city's upscale restaurants, but he was not taken seriously. "[In] New York, I couldn't get a job because I was American," he later recalled. "Chefs were French, German, Swiss. Americans washed dishes." Recognizing that he would have more cooking opportunities if he had classical training in French cooking, Emeril decided to head to France, which was considered the best place to train as a chef. Europe offered him the opportunity to learn what he could about French cuisine.

FRENCH COOKING

Emeril ended up working in France for three months as an unpaid apprentice. He lived and worked first in the city of Lyon. Situated between Paris and Marseille, Lyon is considered the gourmet food capital of the country. Some of France's finest chefs are located in the city. Two of the finest wine growing regions in the country are nearby—Beaujolais to the north and the Côtes du Rhône to the south. Emeril also worked in restaurant kitchens in the French capital city of Paris, which is renowned for its diverse and international cuisines.

Things weren't easy for Emeril in France. The top chefs were very hard on those who worked for them. "You got laughed at, you got yelled at, you got treated wrong," Emeril said in an interview. He told of being pushed and shoved around and forced to do mostly unskilled work. "But that was OK. That was part of it. I didn't speak the language. Didn't make any money." What he did do was learn everything he could.

One of the things Emeril learned was that being a gourmet chef involved more than knowing cooking techniques. A

The medieval architecture of Lyon, France, can be seen in this view from the city's Bellecour plaza. Lyon is the second-largest city in France.

chef provides a dining experience that involves the human senses of taste, smell, and sight. Without the two P's—preparation and presentation—a chef is just a cook. The ingredients in dishes are important, but so are the processes of preparing the meal and its ultimate "plating" before serving.

One of the greatest lessons he learned in France, Emeril has said, is that mastering the skills of food preparation and presentation was not enough. In a successful high-end restaurant, he explains, "Food is an equal part of a little formula that [also] encompasses ambience, service, and a wine

CHEF-OLOGY

The term *chef* covers many job responsibilities in the kitchen of a restaurant. Below are some of most commonly used chef titles and the responsibilities of the position:

Chef de cuisine—the manager of the kitchen and kitchen staff. Responsibilities include determining what goes on the menu, preparing the work schedule and payroll for the entire kitchen staff, and ordering everything from table linens to the vegetable of the day.

Executive chef—the highest-level chef. Executive chefs usually have an educational training diploma, certificate, or degree. These chefs coordinate all functions taking place in the kitchen.

Head chef—the boss in the kitchen. Head chefs have professional cooks who have been hired to work for them.

Sous chef—the second in command in the kitchen. He or she is responsible for the physical operation of the kitchen. These duties include some cooking preparation and the supervision of staff working in the kitchen.

program. Food is only one of the four parts, and no one of those parts is greater than the other parts."

Early on in Emeril's career, he recognized the importance of not only preparing delicious food for restaurant patrons, but also paying attention to everything a customer experiences in the establishment. The ambience of a restaurant, for example, can be affected by the look and feel of the silverware, the cleanliness of the rest rooms, and the quality of the tablecloths and napkins.

BACK IN THE U.S.A

After Emeril returned to the United States, he got a job with Dunfey Hotels. The hotel chain owned and operated hotels in several states, including Massachusetts, Maine, New Hampshire, and New York.

In New York, Emeril worked in Dunfey's Berkshire Place hotel, where Wolfgang Puck was introducing a new style of cooking called "nouvelle cuisine." Also known as California cuisine, it featured dishes that use fresh, light ingredients and require an elaborate presentation. While at the Berkshire, Lagasse said, he learned "how to work on a high-pressure [cooking] line." In an interview he noted that Wolfgang was a perfectionist, who "worked me hard."

Emeril next worked in Massachusetts, in one of Dunfey's Boston hotels, the Parker House. The historic hotel, which opened in 1855, contains the nation's longest continuously operating restaurant. Lagasse worked at the hotel restaurant as a sous chef. Years later he would recall how in 1979 he met Julia Child there when she called him out of the kitchen to compliment him on one of his dishes.

Emeril recognized that knowing how to select wines is an important part of running an upscale establishment, so while

Early in his career, Emeril worked at a Manhattan restaurant run by the Austrian chef Wolfgang Puck. In the late 1970s Puck had become famous for his California cuisine, a style of cooking involves combining elements of diverse cooking styles as well as the use of fresh, organic meats, fruits, and vegetables.

at the Parker House he focused on teaching himself about wine. Every week he purchased an inexpensive bottle of wine and made careful notes about its aroma, taste, and origins in a wine book that he kept. Learning about wine would become one of his hobbies.

In late 1980 Dunfey sent Lagasse as an executive chef to Maine, where its newly named Seasons restaurant, located in a hotel near the Portland Jetport, was struggling financially. He had just turned 21. "It was his first executive chef position," the hotel's former general manager, Fern Genest, would recall later. "He was very creative but limited by corporate structure—I call it corporate interference. Everything he suggested had to be approved through our food and beverage guidelines."

Emeril and Elizabeth settled in Portland with their new daughter Jessica. (A second daughter, Jillian would arrive two years later.) Genest remembers, "He went on about his new baby girl! But, he was serious about his job, putting in long hours—he was there all the time." Emeril's cooking and his successful management of the kitchen soon turned the restaurant around.

In 1980 Dunfey Hotels Corporation owned or managed about 9,000 rooms in hotels located mostly on the East Coast. In 1983 it was reorganized into two separate operating divisions: Dunfey Hotels, which owned hotels and motor inns, and Omni International Hotels, which featured upscale hotels.

Following that success, Lagasse was sent to another Dunfey restaurant, Clancy's, which was located on the trendy "lower end" of Cape Cod, Massachusetts. A popular vacation destination, the Cape features picturesque beaches, quaint shops, and a variety of dining establishments.

A Four-Month Interview

Taking the post at Clancy's proved to be a career-changing move for Emeril. It was at Clancy's in 1982 that a vacationing businessman who recruited candidates in the restaurant industry sampled the young chef's food. He was so impressed with Emeril's cuisine that he told his friend Ella Brennan to consider Lagasse for the position of executive chef at the upscale New Orleans restaurant Commander's Palace.

Ella and her brother, Richard Brennan, were famous in New Orleans for their restaurant empire. The Brennan family operated many restaurants in the city, but the best known was the century-old Commander's Palace. Many people considered it one of the top restaurants in the country. In 1982 the renowned executive chef of Commander's Palace, Paul Prudhomme, was planning to leave to open his own restaurant in New Orleans, K-Paul's. The Brennans needed someone to replace him.

Ella Brennan gave Emeril a call, beginning a four-month-long process of interviewing him. "Every week we would talk," Lagasse explained. "She would say, 'Today, I want to talk about what inspires you. Is bread inspiring you? Is a book inspiring you?' Ella is a genius with people. We would talk for a half hour, 40 minutes. The next Wednesday, the phone would ring: 'Today, I want to talk about your philosophies about people. How do you motivate people?'"

Emeril was just 23 years old, so it was difficult for Ella to consider him for the head chef position at her prestigious restaurant. But after many weeks of talking with Emeril, she decided it was time to interview him in person. She arranged to bring him to New Orleans for a long weekend to meet the rest of the restaurateurs in the family.

It did not take long, once Lagasse arrived, for him to seal the deal. "The enthusiasm, the integrity, the energy, it was all evident," Ella would later say. Before dinner was even finished on Sunday night, both Ella and Dick knew Emeril was going to be the new executive chef at Commander's Palace.

CHAPTER FOUR

THE BIG EASY

Nicknamed "The Big Easy," New Orleans is known for its jazz and blues music, as well as for its festivals, especially the huge annual Mardi Gras. Tourism is a major industry in the city, where both locals and visitors enjoy its hospitality, music, food, and fun.

The southern Louisiana region was inhabited by Choctaw Indians before New Orleans was established as a French colony in the 1690s. The growing city was run by the French from 1718 to 1765, and then by the Spanish from 1765 to 1803. After the Louisiana Purchase was approved in 1803, Louisiana became part of the United States. The descendants of slaves from West Africa lived in the city and surrounding region, and immigrants from Europe and Canada established homes there. The mixture of ethnic groups and cultures resulted in Louisiana cuisine that is considered to be one of a kind.

Tourists walk down a busy street in the historic French Quarter of New Orleans. No one knows for sure where the nickname originated, but some people claim New Orleans is called "The Big Easy" because life is slower, simpler, and more easygoing there than in any other city in the United States.

LOUISIANA CREOLE AND CAJUN CUISINE

During Louisiana's colonial period, the Spanish introduced the word *criollo*, which became *Creole*, to refer to persons of African or European heritage born in the New World. In the 1800s the term was used by Louisianans to identify themselves as native to the region, and not foreign-born or Anglo-American settlers.

The word *Cajun* comes from *Acadian*. Acadia is a region of Canada that included Nova Scotia. Around 1755 a French-speaking group was deported from Acadia by the British. A large number of Acadians settled in the bayous of southwestern Louisiana, where they became known as Cajuns. The Cajuns lived a fairly isolated life, and they typically depended on locally available ingredients such as wild game, seafood, wild vegetation, and herbs for food.

Both Cajun and Creole cuisines are considered traditional Louisiana food. They often use the same ingredients, but even dishes with the same name can taste very different. The French influence is strong in both cuisines, although some people differentiate between the two by referring to Creole cooking as food for city dwellers and Cajun cuisine as country fare. Dishes like barbecue shrimp, trout meuniere, and shrimp remoulade are considered Creole cuisine. Examples of traditional Cajun dishes are crawfish etouffee and smothered chicken. Cajun food is typically cooked up in a big pot and served family style.

Both Cajun and Creole cuisine make use of what Emeril and other chefs call "the holy trinity" of New Orleans cooking: green peppers, onions, and celery.

NEW NEW ORLEANS COOKING

When Emeril headed down to New Orleans, he was just 23 years old. Although he had worked in restaurants in Paris and in various states of the Northeast, he had never experienced living in New Orleans. But he quickly learned about Louisiana traditional cuisines. Many recipes had been passed down from generation to generation for more than 200 years within families of the city. He referred to these dishes as "Old New Orleans."

"When I first arrived in New Orleans in 1983," Emeril said, "everyone was eating Old New Orleans food, meaning wonderful but heavy Creole and Cajun delicacies such as baked, smothered oysters, shrimp remoulade, crabmeat ravigote, stuffed artichokes, thickly rouxed gumbos . . . and bananas Foster. . . . [M]y customers loved eating Old New Orleans. I did, too, but I soon grew bored and started experimenting with both the local palate and with the fresh local food products."

Lagasse respected the New Orleans tradition, but added new ingredients and techniques. He tweaked recipes, combining Cajun and Creole cooking with seasonings and techniques from other cultures. He would later say, "Fusion is what made me what I am now." He referred to these creations as "new New Orleans dishes." He described the dishes as "food whose roots are planted in a solid foundation of Creole heritage, but which has grown through exposure to other exotic cultures; Creole reinvented with an Oriental, Portuguese, or New Mexican flourish."

Emeril brought other changes to Commander's Palace. As executive chef, he mandated that foods be made from scratch and that dishes use only fresh—not canned or frozen—ingredients. He established relationships with growers, arranging

Emeril ran the kitchen at the historic New Orleans restaurant Commander's Palace for seven-and-a-half years.

that they would provide certain products that met his high standards specifically for his restaurant. At Commander's Palace, the kitchen staff made their own cheese and sausages, using meats and milk provided by local farmers. This way he ensured that his restaurant had the freshest produce and specialty foods he wanted. Lagasse also established relationships with local fisherman so he could buy fresh fish and quality shellfish directly from them.

SUCCESS AND FAILURE

Commander's Palace flourished. As a chef, Lagasse was a great success. "Once Emeril got down here, we really had a chemistry. It worked," Ella Brennan told CNN. About his decision to take the chance in New Orleans, Emeril would

New Orleans Cuisine

andouille—a New Orleans–style spicy sausage, typically used to make jambalaya, red beans and rice, and other New Orleans dishes.

bananas Foster—a dessert consisting of cooked bananas, vanilla ice cream, and a sauce containing alcohol, which is ignited as a flambé when served.

beignet—a square-shaped fried dough sprinkled with confectioners' sugar.

boudin—a spicy Cajun sausage made of pork, pig's blood, pork fat, and other ingredients such as rice, chopped onions, and breadcrumbs.

bread pudding—a dessert made from bread soaked in a mixture of milk, eggs, and sugar, that is baked and served covered with a rich, sweet sauce.

crawfish—crustaceans that resemble small lobsters, known locally as "mudbugs"; often served highly seasoned and boiled with onions, new potatoes, garlic, and sausage.

etouffee—a simmered roux-based gravy or sauce served over rice.

filé powder—ground sassafras leaves, used to thicken gumbo.

gumbo—a type of stew or soup thickened with okra or rice and featuring a rich roux and seafood or sausage.

jambalaya—a spicy dish made with rice, tomato, and seafood or meat such as andouille (based on the Spanish dish paella).

maque choux—an American Indian and Acadian French side dish of corn, green bell pepper, tomatoes, and onions.

okra—from West Africa, a vegetable used in gumbo.

remoulade—a red, sharp dressing or sauce made with egg, oil and vinegar, paprika, and various flavorings.

roux—from French, a base for dishes made from flour and oil or butter.

later say, "I guess I feel that I was following my instincts and at the same time being guided by the best. I became totally intrigued with Louisiana, the people the food. It is a part of my life."

But his marriage did not survive the relocation to New Orleans. Immersed in work at the restaurant, Emeril lived there 18 hours a day and had little time to give to his family. Soon after arriving in the city, Elizabeth decided to return to Massachusetts along with their two daughters, Jessica and Jillian. In 1986 the marriage officially ended in divorce.

TAKING RISKS

Lagasse worked as executive chef at Commander's Palace for seven and a half years. When he decided the time was right to open his own restaurant, he chose to stay in the city. But Emeril moved out of the Garden District, the site of Commander's Palace, to the Warehouse District, located on the edge of the French Quarter.

The Warehouse District is one of New Orleans' oldest neighborhoods. It was a busy industrial area during the 1800s, when grain, coffee, and produce were shipped through the nearby Port of New Orleans on the Mississippi. But in the 1980s, much of the area had been abandoned by businesses, and it contained many empty buildings and warehouses.

Today, the Warehouse District, which is also known as the New Orleans Arts District, houses numerous studios, boutiques, museums, art galleries, and upscale eateries.

Some people considered the Warehouse District to be prime for redevelopment. The city's Contemporary Arts Center had opened there in 1976, and the area was beginning to attract artists of various disciplines, including music, dance, photography, sculpture, and painting. In 1984 a federal tax incentive was offered to keep revitalization of the area going. The tax incentive attracted numerous business and real estate developers. One of them was RCB Builders, owned by Henry Lambert. He bought one of the warehouses and renovated its upper floors as apartments.

Emeril had been at Commander's Palace for a little more than a year when Lambert bought the warehouse. The developer frequented Commander's Palace, and he often encouraged Emeril to open a restaurant on the first floor of Lambert's renovated building. In 1989, with an established following and a reputation as one of the finest chefs in New Orleans, Emeril decided to take the risk of opening his own place—in an area where it was considered dangerous to walk after dark.

A barrier to moving forward with the restaurant was its location in a neighborhood that was not considered safe. Most high-end restaurants were in the French Quarter or Garden District. Many banks turned down Emeril's request for a loan. He worked for eight months developing a business plan, proposed budget, dining and kitchen design, and even a wine list, before he could convince a bank to give him a loan.

Around the same time Lagasse took another risk in deciding to marry again. In 1989 he and Tari Hohn, an actress and fashion designer, were married. She worked with him in creating the interior design of his new fine-dining restaurant. It had features such as a high ceiling, exposed brick, hardwood floors, and an open kitchen. After the loan came through, construction began that year.

In January 1990 Lagasse and business partner Eric Linquest founded Emeril's Homebase to run the business operations for the restaurant. Linquest served as president of the company, which was based in New Orleans.

EMERIL'S RESTAURANT

On March 26, 1990, Emeril's opened its doors. Located on Tchoupitoulas (pronounced "chop-it-TOO-las") Street, the restaurant was an instant hit. Within 30 minutes of opening, there was a 90-minute wait for a table.

The menu featured Lagasse's new New Orleans cooking—Creole cuisine fused with elements of Southwestern, Asian, or Portuguese ethnic influences. Lagasse continued to follow

Emeril Lagasse holds plates of Oysters Julia (left) and Darian's Chicken and Waffles (right) at Emeril's Restaurant in New Orleans. He opened his first restaurant in March 1990.

the "fresh ingredients, local foods" policy he had established at Commander's Palace. At Emeril's, members of the kitchen staff were instructed to use only the finest and freshest products available. Top-quality ingredients came directly from local ranchers, farmers, and fishermen. Emeril's signature dishes included New Orleans barbecue shrimp, grilled double cut Niman Ranch pork chops, and banana cream pie. They continue to be signature dishes today.

The new restaurant and its chef received much praise. In its first year, the new eatery was dubbed "Restaurant of the Year" by *Esquire* magazine food critic John Mariani. In 1991 Lagasse was named "Best Southeast Regional Chef" by the James Beard Foundation. And in May 1994 *Restaurants and Institutions* magazine bestowed its Ivy Award on the restaurant.

NOLA

Lagasse opened a second restaurant in the city, this time in the French Quarter, in October 1992. Called NOLA (*NO* stands for New Orleans and *LA* for Louisiana), the casual restaurant in a modern two-story building featured Creole and Acadian cuisine but with influences of Southern, Southwestern, and Vietnamese cooking. Emeril explained at the time that at NOLA he was "trying to bring back honest Cajun-Creole cooking."

Like Emeril's, NOLA highlighted regional specialties. The new restaurant featured foods such as boudin sausage (a Cajun specialty of a pork casing filled with pork, pig's liver, and rice)

In October 1999 Emeril's Restaurant won the Grand Award given by *Wine Spectator* magazine.

and jambalaya pizza (made with chicken andouille, shrimp, cheese, and smoked tomato sauce). In 1993 the new restaurant also earned *Esquire*'s "Restaurant of the Year" award.

TV TIME

In 1992 Lagasse's reputation gained him an appearance on the PBS series *Great Chefs*. The program brought viewers into the kitchens of chefs as they worked in their restaurant kitchens. On the show, the chefs shared techniques, regional recipes, and culinary tips.

A year later, in October 1993, Emeril appeared on Julia Child's PBS show *Cooking with Master Chefs*. In the series, Child visited 16 chefs in the United States and discussed their regional specialties. One of them was Emeril. In the program featuring Lagasse, she referred to the Massachusetts native as the "quintessential New Orleans chef" and praised his two New Orleans restaurants. For the show, Emeril prepared shrimp etouffee and a traditional Louisiana crab and crawfish boil.

In April 1993 Lagasse shared his more creative approach to Creole cuisine when he published his first cookbook, *Emeril's New New Orleans Cooking*. That summer he went on his first national book tour.

EMERIL'S NEW ORLEANS FISH HOUSE

In November 1995 Lagasse opened his third restaurant. This one was named for his adopted city, but not located in it. Emeril's New Orleans Fish House was in the MGM Grand Hotel and Casino in Las Vegas, Nevada. Like his other restaurants, it featured Emeril's "new New Orleans" style of cooking. Its menu offered a lighter version of Creole cuisine based on fresh seafood and shellfish from Louisiana as well as from the West Coast.

Emeril was invited to join the fledgling Food Network in 1993, and soon became the network's biggest star. His enthusiasm made Emeril a national celebrity and helped raise interest in his restaurants and cookbooks.

CHAPTER FIVE

CELEBRITY CHEF

In July 1993 Emeril Lagasse was asked by the Television Food Network (TVFN), a new specialty cable channel, to host a cooking show. The idea of being on television appealed to him. "For the previous four years, I'd been doing 12 shifts a week on the line," he explained. "Closing the restaurant at three o'clock, four o'clock in the morning, waiting for the cleanup crew. . . . I thought about the TV thing and it seemed like almost going back to school. That excited me."

Emeril also liked the idea of helping people take an interest in what they ate. He said that he was "just wanting to influence at least one person a day to be a little interested in food and cooking. If I did that, then hey, I could say that I've done my food deed of the day"

But Emeril's first show for the Television Food Network, *How to Boil Water*, was not successful. Neither was the second attempt, called *Emeril and Friends*. Neither scripted show attracted much of an audience. However, executives at the network, which was renamed the Food Network, still believed that Emeril Lagasse had potential.

THE ESSENCE OF EMERIL

The third show that Emeril created proved to be a winner. Called *The Essence of Emeril*, it began taping in August 1994. Lagasse still wanted to run his restaurants, so he would fly to New York City every week to tape a week's worth of episodes in two days. It was a crazy schedule, he explained: "I'd be in the restaurant Saturday night till 4 A.M., on an airplane at seven, get off the airplane at 11:30, be in the studio at one, shooting four shows on Sunday afternoon—my day off. I mean, fried to a crisp." Emeril filmed his shows on Sunday and Monday, then turned around and went back to New Orleans. He was paid $300 per episode. The shows were not scripted, which allowed Emeril to be himself in front of the camera.

When *The Essence of Emeril* debuted in November 1994, it was an immediate hit. Food Network president Erica Gruen explained in 1998, "From the beginning, Emeril was a true television original. Intimate and passionate, he shot energy straight through the camera and out the other side. People were fascinated by his exquisite food and impeccable technique, wrapped in a package of high-voltage intensity. The man just packed a wallop, TV-wise."

Viewers loved Emeril's quick wit and enthusiastic banter, as well as his catchphrases "Bam!" and "Kick it up a notch." The trademark exclamation "Bam!" originated, he has explained, to keep the crew awake while taping five or six shows a day. After long hours of shooting, crewmembers would get sleepy. So as Emeril added ingredients to dishes, he would suddenly yell "Bam!" He explained, "It was like, BAM! to wake everybody up. And then, I've got everybody's attention. And that's how it started, and it kind of evolved from there."

Thanks to his popular and educational shows, Emeril has been nominated eight times for a Daytime Emmy Award, which is considered one of the most prestigious awards a television performer can win. However, Emeril has not yet taken home the award.

The Essence of Emeril became one of the network's highest rated shows. In its December 23, 1996, issue *Time* magazine included the show in its list of "The Best Television of 1996."

REEVALUATING

However, amid the restaurant business pressures and his growing celebrity, Emeril found his second marriage was failing. He was so focused on his career that he had little time for anything else. By 1995 he and Tari were in the midst of a divorce. It became official the following year.

THE FOOD NETWORK

April 1993 saw the launch of Television Food Network (TVFN), which would later be known simply as the Food Network. Founded by G. P. Reese Schonfeld, who had cofounded CNN in the 1980s, the new network began with just a few shows in its lineup, including Lagasse's *The Essence of Emeril*. Other early programs were hosted by Jacques Pépin, David Rosengarten, Donna Hanover, and Curtis Aikens. In 1994 the network acquired the rights to reruns of the hit Julia Child program *The French Chef*, and the Food Network quickly took off. In 1997 E. W. Scripps Company acquired the channel.

Food Network divides its programming into two segments. Daytime programs are mainly how-to cooking shows, including favorites like *Everyday Italian*, *30 Minute Meals*, and *Paula's Best Dishes*. Nighttime programming is devoted to food-related shows such as *Diners, Drive-Ins and Dives*, or reality competitions such as *The Next Iron Chef* and *The Great Food Truck Race*.

In 1993, when Food Network first aired, early audience numbers were low, at around 6.5 million. Food Network launched in international markets in 2009 and can now be seen by viewers in more than 10 countries. In 2011 more than 96 million U.S. households had access to Food Network and more than 7 million people visited the network's website every month.

Emeril is pictured at the center of this gathering of popular Food Network chefs. He has been one of the network's biggest stars since the mid-1990s.

In an interview he gave around that time, Lagasse admitted that being in the restaurant business made it hard to maintain relationships. "It's a very demanding schedule, the hours, the holidays," he said. "It's very tough on family life and relationships. It's a very demanding and grueling business." His average workday, he said, was 15 to 16 hours a day.

Daughter Jessica would later say about her father, "I think that after his second divorce, he took a step back and sort of had to reevaluate and reposition himself and figure out what he needed."

EMERIL LIVE!

But Emeril did not slow down. In fact, he soon had more to do. In January 1997 he began taping a new show, *Emeril Live!* Once a month Lagasse would fly to New York from New Orleans, where he would spend a few days taping three shows a day, from around 2 P.M. to 8:30 P.M. on Tuesday, Wednesday, Thursday, and Friday.

The hour-long program, which debuted later that month, was taped before a live studio audience and included a four-member band. Its format gave Emeril even more freedom to be spontaneous. He interacted with the members of his audience, who responded with enthusiasm to his energetic cooking style as well as his wisecracks, catchphrases, and flair for the dramatic.

On his shows Emeril encouraged people to get creative with food by using recipes as a guide rather than as instructions set in concrete. "I'm just not into following 'food law,'" he said in an interview. "You have to be flexible." In other words, people shouldn't be afraid of "kicking it up a notch"— improving dishes by making their flavor more intense—typically by adding garlic or his special spice blend, Emeril's

Essence. He would tell people that cooking "ain't rocket science," and that they could do it, too.

Not everyone liked the theatrics on *Emeril Live!* The founder of *Food Arts* magazine, Michael Batterberry, told food writer Amanda Hesser of the *New York Times*, "A lot of professional foodies are a bit dismayed at the tone of the program. It really smacks a little bit of the wrestling ring or the roller derby." Hesser agreed. She and other critics complained that during his shows Emeril seldom gave specific measurements and that his instructions were often vague. The critics wanted more instruction and less entertainment.

Everyone else raved about *Emeril Live!*, however. And the show continued to grow in popularity. When it was taped in cities outside New York, such as Philadelphia and Chicago, *Emeril Live!* drew huge crowds. In 1997 the *New York Daily News* called Emeril Lagasse "one of the tube's most smokin' personalities." That same year a *People* magazine story noted that "the 28 million viewers of the Food Network—which carries his daily *Emeril Live!* and frequent reruns of his *The Essence of Emeril* cooking shows—send him about 7,000 letters a week." In 1997 *Emeril Live!* won a Cable Ace Award for Best Informational Show.

COOKBOOKS

In addition to hosting popular cooking shows, Lagasse published several cookbooks that became bestsellers. His second cookbook, *Louisiana Real and Rustic*, appeared in September 1996. The following September saw the publication of *Emeril's Creole Christmas*.

A fourth book, *Emeril's TV Dinners*, was released in September 1998. It featured a collection of Lagasse's favorite recipes from his Food Network programs, categorized under such chapter titles as "Fall River Memories," "Emerilized Starters," and "Pork Fat Rules." The next year saw the release of *Every Day's a Party: Louisiana Recipes for Celebrating with Family and Friends.*

Lagasse publicized his new publications on book tours, and his television fans flocked to his book signings. By 2000 Emeril's books had sold 2 million copies.

FOOD CORRESPONDENT

Meanwhile Lagasse was appearing on television in another venue. In January 1998 *Good Morning America* (*GMA*) hired him as a food correspondent. In an interview, he clarified that in this role he would do more than present recipes from his cookbooks, although he did that, too.

As a food correspondent, Lagasse explained, "I can impart my knowledge beyond just chicken dish of the week. It is a real opportunity to educate people about food. I have done segments on everything from buying eggs to cooking with oils. People take this stuff for granted, but there's a lot to learn." More than 12 years later, the partnership with *GMA* would still be going strong.

EMERIL'S DELMONICO

In 1998 Emeril opened a fourth restaurant, back in New Orleans. He had been approached the previous year by the

In May 2000 Emeril Lagasse appeared on *Who Wants to Be a Millionaire*. He donated his $125,000 winnings to a children's charity in New Orleans.

owners of Delmonico, a restaurant in the New Orleans Garden District. Delmonico was one of the country's oldest restaurants, founded in 1895, and was famous for serving traditional Creole cuisine.

The restaurant had been in the Brown family for several generations when sisters Angela Brown and Rose Brown Deitrich asked Emeril to take over the business. He bought it from them in 1997. His goal, he would say, was to preserve the classic style of Creole cuisine and dining. He told an interviewer, "We're going to bring back a bit of the grander New Orleans traditional family dining that's being lost in the city."

The elegant two-story building was reopened in June 1998 as Emeril's Delmonico. In 2002 it received the AAA Four Diamond Award, the Mobil Four Star Award, and *Wine Spectator's* Best of Award of Excellence.

Chef Emeril also garnered praise. In May 1998 the National Restaurant Association awarded him the Salute to Excellence Award. That October GQ magazine dubbed him Chef of the Year. And in December 1998 *People* magazine selected him as one of its "25 Most Intriguing People of the Year." The accompanying story pointed out that tickets to *Emeril Live!* were extremely hard to come by. Around 1,500 tickets were being requested for each show, and the studio audience was set at 150.

GROWING EMERIL'S EMPIRE

In 1999 Emeril opened two more restaurants. February saw the opening of Emeril's Orlando at Universal Studios, in CityWalk, in Florida. The following May Delmonico Steakhouse opened its doors in the Venetian Resort Hotel Casino in Las Vegas. It would win the Grand Award by *Wine Spectator* in 2004.

Emeril also established himself as a brand in 1999, when he partnered with All-Clad Metalcrafters to create Emerilware, a line of high-quality, gourmet cookware. The following year, he made a deal with B&G Foods to put his name on a gourmet food line called Emeril's Original. The food products included marinades, seasonings, salad dressing, and pasta sauces, as well as his spice blend Essence.

More opportunities arose. In June 2002 Lagasse partnered with cutlery manufacturer Wusthof-Trident to launch Emerilware knives. The following year he worked in partnership with Sanita Clogs of Denmark, to introduce a new line of clogs called Emeril by Sanita.

A less-successful venture was starring in a sitcom for NBC. September 2001 saw the release of a new comedy starring Emeril Lagasse as the host of a cooking show, much like the one he did for Food Network. NBC's *Emeril* lasted just 13 episodes before the program was pulled. However, millions of Americans who had not seen him on his cooking shows now knew who he was.

COOKING WITH KIDS

Lagasse wrote more cookbooks. In September 2001, he released his sixth book, *Prime Time Emeril*. The next year he published a cookbook for kids. Released in March 2002, Emeril's *There's a Chef in My Soup! Recipes for the Kid in Everyone* was dedicated to his daughters, Jessica and Jillian, and to his "young fans and friends." The colorfully illustrated cookbook featured 75 kid-tested recipes presented in easy-to-follow directions. Within two weeks of its release it was a *New York Times* bestseller.

In 2003 the Emerilware line was expanded to include quality bakeware such as cake pans and cookie sheets. At that time, Emeril introduced a line of cookware for kids—it included a saucepan and a child-sized spoon, ladle, and turner. The set also featured an apron, "Baby Bam Spice," and a copy of *There's a Chef in My Soup!*

MORE RESTAURANTS

Two more new restaurants made an appearance that year, both in Florida. In January 2003 Emeril opened his seventh restaurant, Emeril's Tchoup Chop at Universal Orlando's Royal Pacific Resort (later renamed Loews Royal Pacific Resort at Universal Orlando). The name Tchoup Chop, pronounced "chop chop," comes from Tchoupitoulas Street, where Emeril's original restaurant is located in New Orleans.

The following November, Emeril's Miami Beach opened at the Lowes Miami Beach Hotel. The elaborate 8,000-square-foot restaurant featured Lagasse's signature dishes such as New Orleans barbecue shrimp and Niman Ranch pork chops.

Emeril's Atlanta in the Buckhead district of Atlanta, Georgia, also opened in 2003. However, that restaurant closed five years later, in 2008.

FAMILY MATTERS

In the 1990s, after working more than 30 years for the textile company in Fall River, Emeril's father retired. Both John and Hilda moved to New Orleans, where they made their home. "Mr. John" worked in Emeril's restaurants on an as-needed

In June 2004 *Restaurants and Institutions* magazine named Lagasse "Executive of the Year."

basis, while Hilda occasionally made appearances on his television shows. Like her son, she quickly learned about New Orleans food and served it up to him at family meals.

Around 1998 Emeril began dating Alden Lovelace, a real estate agent who managed the condo complex he lived in. The two had known each other for many years as her family frequented Emeril's Restaurant. In May 2000, 40-year-old Emeril married for a third time. He and Alden, a 33-year-old native of Gulfport, Mississippi, enjoyed a small private ceremony in New Orleans, followed by a Louisiana-style dance party with around 500 guests at one of Emeril's restaurants.

In March 2003 the couple had a son, Emeril John Lagasse IV, whom they nicknamed E. J. A year and a half later, in

Emeril and wife Alden with their daughter Meril at a 2006 event.

December 2004, they had a daughter, Meril Lovelace Lagasse. Meril bears her father's name, minus the first "E."

The family lived in New Orleans, but Alden and Emeril also had a family weekend home built in Pass Christian, Mississippi, a Gulf coast community near Gulfport and about an hour away from New Orleans.

FOOD NETWORK STAR

In May 2003 Lagasse signed a five-year, multimillion-dollar contract with the E. W. Scripps Company, which had assumed ownership of the Food Network. *Emeril Live!* was the Food Network's top-rated show, and the network agreed to produce 90 more episodes. It also agreed to produce 26 episodes per year of *The Essence of Emeril*, as well as several network specials featuring the chef.

In a press release, Food Network president Judy Girard called Lagasse "the cornerstone of the network." The deal with the Food Network also included international rights, which meant that viewers in countries other than the United States and Canada could now watch Lagasse's two Food Network shows.

Emeril continued to produce bestselling books. In October 2003, he released his eighth book, *From Emeril's Kitchens*. A ninth book—his second children's cookbook—hit the bookstores the following April. Emeril's *There's a Chef in My Family: Recipes to Get Everybody Cooking* emphasized having people cook together as a family.

Later in 2004 Emeril released his tenth cookbook. Called *Emeril's Potluck: Comfort Food with a Kicked-Up Attitude*, it featured simple recipes useful for feeding large groups of people.

THE EMERIL BRAND

Numerous companies continued to express interest in form-ing partnerships with Emeril Lagasse. In March 2004 he made a deal with Hillshire Farms of Sara Lee Food to launch Emeril's Gourmet Meats. At the same time he also expanded his product line with All-Clad, launching the Emerilware Electric Appliance Collection and Emerilware Cast Iron Cookware. The following May he joined with California-based Pride of San Juan to launch Emeril's Gourmet Produce, a line of lettuce salad blends, fresh herbs, and heir-loom tomatoes. In 2005 Lagasse joined with Waterford Wedgwood to produce Emeril Professional, a line of high quality stoneware.

Whether he was selling salad dressing and pasta sauce (B&G Foods) or frozen shrimp (New Orleans Fish House), Lagasse was adamant that he believed in the products that carried his name. "Whatever it is, I'm going to be totally involved," he told an interviewer in 2005. "It's never about, 'OK, here's the name.' Even if it comes down to doing a Crest commercial, I'm going to dictate who's going to be involved. I'm going to have final creative say, or I'm not going to do it."

After Hurricane Katrina devastated the Gulf coast in 2005, Emeril was faced with the daunting task of reopening his badly damaged New Orleans restaurants.

CHAPTER SIX

REBUILDING

In August 2005 Lagasse owned nine award-winning restaurants—three in New Orleans. He had authored numerous bestselling cookbooks and had flourishing business ventures. He was a well-known television personality who had taped more than 1,500 shows for the Food Network. Emeril was earning around $9 million a year in profits from his nine restaurants and his many licensing agreements. But at the end of August Hurricane Katrina struck New Orleans, and Emeril's empire received a major blow.

RESTAURANT BLUES

Emeril wasn't alone. The economic blow to the region was tremendous. Before Katrina, Louisiana's restaurant industry was the largest employer in the state, generating $5.2 billion in sales per year.

In New Orleans hundreds of restaurants were devastated by the storm. Even those that emerged relatively undamaged from the winds and flooding could not reopen right away because damaged city pipes were taking in contaminated ground water. Workers had to ensure the water they used was safe to drink by boiling it on the stove—if they had the power to run appliances.

And in most cases the restaurants had no workers. Chefs, waiters, line cooks, and dishwashers had become refugees. They no longer had places to live, schools for their children, or open restaurants in which to work in New Orleans. Many who left the area before the storm did not return afterward.

NEW ORLEANS SPIRIT

In October 2005, Lagasse got some negative press in New Orleans when he went on a publicity tour for his 11th cookbook, *Emeril's Delmonico: A Restaurant with a Past*. The book, which featured recipes for the Creole dishes served at the restaurant, came out just weeks after Katrina struck.

Ever the businessman, Emeril stuck to his scheduled book tour. As he visited various cities, he continued to express his commitment to rebuilding New Orleans and restoring its reputation as a culinary leader. He insisted that the people would ensure the city's comeback. "They won't lose the spirit, they won't lose the soul," he said in an October interview with National Public Radio. "People are discussing at lunch what they're gonna have for dinner—that's the spirit of New Orleans. And it can't be blown away."

Emeril was displaying some of that spirit himself. He had to deal with damage to his home in New Orleans caused by Katrina, as well as the total destruction of the second home he and Alden had just moved into in Pass Christian.

CARNIVALE DU VIN FUNDRAISER

That month his foundation held a major fundraiser. A few years earlier, in September 2002, Lagasse had created a non-

Hurricane Katrina caused an estimated $125 billion in damage to the Gulf coast of the United States, making it the most costly hurricane in history.

DEAD END

Before Hurricane Katrina, the tourist industry in Louisiana provided jobs for 85,000 people and pumped about $5.6 billion into the economy.

profit charitable organization in his name. The Emeril Lagasse Foundation was intended to provide funds and support for educational opportunities and programs for disadvantaged children in communities where his restaurants operated.

The Foundation had been scheduled to hold its first major fundraiser in the fall of 2005. The event was supposed to take place in New Orleans, but Hurricane Katrina and Hurricane Rita, which blew through town in September, forced a change of plans. The fundraiser was moved to Las Vegas.

Held on October 29, the relocated Carnivale du Vin brought together many big names in the culinary and wine world. Tickets to the black tie charity gala cost $1,000 each. At the fundraiser ticketholders had the opportunity to eat a multicourse gourmet meal and participate in an auction that offered items such as lunch and tennis lessons with tennis pro Andre Agassi.

It was a difficult time to run a fundraising event, but in the wake of Katrina, many people wanted to help, the foundation's executive director, Kristen Shannon said. "So many chefs were calling Emeril asking what could be done," she explained. Ultimately 120 chefs signed up to help out. They included celebrity chefs Mario Batali and Daniel Boulud. The Venetian Resort Hotel and Casino donated space for the event.

In the aftermath of Katrina, the focus was to benefit the children of New Orleans. Some of the money raised was intended for St. Michael's Special School, a city school that serves children with special needs. Other recipients of the first fundraiser were Second Harvest Food Bank of New Orleans Kid's Café and Covenant House's Covenant Café. In the years that followed, the Carnivale du Vin would serve as an annual fundraising event for the Emeril Lagasse Foundation.

REBUILDING RESTAURANTS

Despite the negative press he received for not reopening his restaurants right away, Lagasse wanted to rebuild his businesses on his own terms. He had standards. He refused to reopen his restaurants without the proper equipment. For that reason, it took him a while to get them up and running.

All three restaurants needed new refrigeration units for the kitchens and the units had to be specially fabricated. That took time. "You can't buy this stuff at Home Depot," Lagasse told the *New York Times*. "I couldn't reopen with a bunch of coolers and propane stoves."

Emeril's Delmonico, which is housed in a building that is more than a century old, would remain closed for more than a year because it had received extensive damage. It would not reopen until after an estimated $500,000 in repairs.

Some losses were not covered by insurance. Emeril's restaurants—and many other upscale eateries in New Orleans—lost the contents of their wine cellars, or suffered serious damage to their wines, because there was no electricity to keep the bottles cool. After the storm, electrical power in the city was out for several weeks while temperatures hovered in the 90s. The heat damaged and destroyed many restaurant wine cellars. In an interview with the Associated Press, the president of Emeril's corporation, Eric Linquest, would later estimate the cost of replacing the company's restaurant wines at more than $700,000.

Linquest would also note, "We spent easily a million dollars getting the restaurants back in shape. And overnight a third of the revenue of the company disappeared."

A SLOW SUMMER

The following summer journalists visiting New Orleans reported that the city was still in bad shape. In August 2006 a writer for *USA Today* noted that owners of tourist-driven businesses like gift shops and boutique hotels were saying that business was off by at least 60 percent compared to the previous summer.

Before Katrina, the city was attracting 10 million visitors a year, typically to the French Quarter, the Garden District, and the Warehouse and Arts District. The number of visitors had sharply declined and businesses were suffering.

To kick off the 2006–07 school year on a positive note for New Orleans students, Lagasse joined with jazz musician Wynton Marsalis to host an educational cooking concert they called Cookin' with Music. The event, which took place on August 28 at the Ernest N. Morial Convention Center, was free of charge for 4,000 school children in the New Orleans area.

In May 2006 Emeril Lagasse was inducted into the MenuMasters Hall of Fame. Each year the editors of *Nation's Restaurant News* select a chef for the Hall. Other members include Paul Prudhomme and Wolfgang Puck.

OTHER CELEBRITY CHEFS

Julia Child (1912–2004): A pioneer in the celebrity chef industry, Child made French gourmet cooking accessible to Americans through her now-classic cookbook *Mastering the Art of French Cooking*. Her first TV program, *The French Chef* (1963–1973), was the most widely broadcast cooking show of its time. Among her other TV shows were *Julia Child and Company*, *Cooking with Master Chefs*, and *Julia and Jacques Cooking at Home*.

Mario Batali (b. 1960): The classically trained Batali is an expert on the history and culture of Italian cuisine. His most well-known TV program was *Molto Mario*, which aired on the Food Network from 1997 to 2007. Batali co-owns restaurants in New York, Las Vegas, and other cities.

Bobby Flay (b. 1964): Known for his *Throwdown!* shows with fellow chefs, Flay is equally renowned for dynamic dishes that emphasize grilling, glazes, relishes, and spicy sauces with a Southwestern flavor. He has hosted nine cooking shows and specials on the Food Network and has appeared on *Emeril Live!*

Rachael Ray (b. 1968): Charming viewers with her own catchy kitchen terms such as "delish," and "yum-o," Ray often maintains that she is a cook, not a chef. Having received no formal culinary training, she has nevertheless earned a broad fan base with programs such as *$40 a Day*, *30-Minute Meals*, and *Rachael Ray's Week in a Day*. She also produces a monthly magazine, *Every Day with Rachael Ray*.

During the stage performance Lagasse and Marsalis educated and entertained as they shared their love and knowledge of cooking and music. They explored themes such as the basic fundamentals and cultural similarities of both crafts, and then moved on to improvisation and the need for creativity in both culinary and musical art forms.

NASA astronaut Jeff Williams holds a packet of food near the galley of the International Space Station (ISS). "It's an absolute honor to share my food with you on such a journey," Emeril told ISS expedition 13 crew Williams, Pavel Vinogradov, and Thomas Reiter in August 2006. "Since I was a little boy, I've been a huge fan of the space program." Williams responded that the crew was pleased with the chef's food. "We sampled the food and especially enjoyed the jambalaya and the kicked up mashed potatoes," Williams said, "in particular, the extra spiciness."

OUT OF THIS WORLD

The same month Emeril received a special honor when he became the first celebrity chef to create meals for NASA astronauts and have those recipes served in space. The crew of the International Space Station received a meal designed by Lagasse and delivered by space shuttle. The crew then talked with the celebrity chef during a special hookup carried live on NASA television.

The five dishes included Emeril's Mardi Gras jambalaya, mashed potatoes with bacon, green beans with garlic, rice pudding, and mixed fruit. The recipients of the celebrity chef's meal were NASA astronaut Jeff Williams, Russian cosmonaut Pavel Vinogradov, and European Space Agency astronaut Thomas Reiter.

OF THIS WORLD

A few months later Lagasse was talking about issues back on earth, in publicizing his latest cookbook, *There's a Chef in My World: Recipes That Take You Places*. The recipes highlighted international dishes such as latkes, huevos rancheros, egg drop soup, linguine Bolognese—as well as Emeril's B.L.T. hotdogs. The dishes were intended for parents to make with their kids.

During a book tour, Lagasse stressed the importance of parents talking to their kids. "From a food perspective, we don't take the time to educate and teach," he said in an interview with the *Dallas Morning News*. "And it all starts at the top, with parents. Just explain to a child what couscous is, for example, or take a simple taco and tell them where it comes from."

Lagasse also stated his belief in the effectiveness of using food to bring families together. He said that in his family Sunday night was family dinner night, a special time for family members to cook, talk, and eat together. "I know we're all busy, but we have to take the time to be a family at the table," he noted.

REBUILDING ON THE GULF COAST

In June 2007, Emeril's Homebase opened a new restaurant, Emeril's Gulf Coast Fish House, at the Island View Casino Resort in Gulfport, Mississippi. The resort is located in an area that had been devastated by Katrina. The new eatery was a sister restaurant to the award-winning Emeril's New Orleans Fish House in Las Vegas.

The opening of the restaurant held special significance for Emeril. Earlier, when he had announced plans for opening the new restaurant, he had said, "I receive offers every day to build new restaurants all over the world, but I chose to open a restaurant on the Gulf coast because it means a lot to me to be a part of the rebuilding of this community. My family and I have very close ties here—my wife Alden grew up in Gulfport and we have spent a lot of time with our family and friends here."

Unfortunately the venture would not do well. Within three years Emeril would have to make the painful announcement that he was shutting down the restaurant.

TABLE 10

A more successful venture would be Table 10, a new restaurant opened in February 2008 at The Palazzo Las Vegas Resort Hotel. Table 10 is named after the table at his flagship restaurant, Emeril's, where he and his team would do their daily planning.

Table 10 featured New American cuisine, which one reviewer described as "comfort food, gone slightly gourmet."

She went on to praise the new eatery for its "casual, approachable vibe and genuine hospitality."

End of an Era

The previous fall, when Table 10 was still in the planning stages, Emeril was told that his show *Emeril Live!* would be ending. In late November, the Food Network announced it planned to cease production on December 11. Food Network publicist Carrie Welch explained that Emeril remained under contract with the Food Network and that it would continue producing *The Essence of Emeril*. Lagasse would also play a part in Food Network specials in the future.

The Food Network publicist provided a statement that Lagasse had prepared: "I am deeply appreciative," he said, "to all the unbelievable staff—many who have been with the show since the beginning—and all the loyal viewers, and the many talented guests who have appeared on the show through the years."

Emeril Live! continued to be seen in reruns on the Fine Living Network, which in May 2010 was rebranded as the Cooking Channel and launched in 57 million homes. A sister channel to the Food Network, it features more instructional programming, while the Food Network emphasizes more reality television and competitive cooking shows.

Emeril poses with Martha Stewart on the set of her radio show, 2008. That year the doyenne of "gracious living" spent $50 million to purchase the rights to Emeril's cookbooks, television shows, and kitchen products.

CHAPTER SEVEN

CHANGING TIMES

In February 2008 the media and merchandising company owned by Martha Stewart announced that it had reached an agreement with Emeril Lagasse to acquire parts of his media and merchandising business. The sale was finalized two months later.

Martha Stewart Living Omnimedia (MSLO) bought the rights to Emeril's television shows, cookbooks, website (www.emerils.com), and his licensed kitchen and food products. The price was $45 million in cash and $5 million in stock. The agreement did not include Emeril's restaurants, corporate office, and foundation-related holdings.

In a press release Lagasse explained the reason for the sale. "We have been able to create a successful and diverse business under the Emeril brand, and with this new venture we can take it to the next level," he said. "By affiliating with a larger company with means, infrastructure and reach, we know we can maximize its great potential."

At the same time Stewart released a statement praising Emeril. "His remarkable talents in the kitchen and his high-energy exuberance delight and inform," she said. "He made television cooking programs mainstream, opening the category to new audiences and proving that cooking is something everyone can enjoy."

A couple of years later, in an interview with the Associated Press, Lagasse would comment optimistically on the sale of his assets to Martha Stewart. "She showed up at a tough time when I thought the whole ship might be going down," he admitted. "Basically, what I have now is a business partner.

That partnership meant that Lagasse began working out of an office at the MSLO New York City headquarters. There, he has a company called Emeril Brand at Martha Stewart Living Omnimedia, which he heads as founder and president.

In June 2008 Emeril unveiled a new column for *Everyday Food*, the cooking magazine published by Martha Stewart Living Omnimedia. He and Martha appeared on the magazine cover, in honor of the new regular column called "Kick It Up—Everyday with Emeril."

EMERIL GREEN

Not long after, a new original series called *Emeril Green* launched on a new specialty channel, the eco-lifestyle network Planet Green. It would be the first of more than a half dozen new programs that Lagasse would host in the coming years.

Produced by After Five Productions, the same company that handled *Emeril Live!*, the new series emphasizes the use of fresh, organic, locally grown foods—a philosophy that Lagasse has been committed to for decades in his restaurants and home kitchen. On various episodes of *Emeril Green*, he

MARTHA STEWART

Martha Stewart is a multitalented entrepreneur, whose successful career has included a catering company that she began in her basement, writing recipe books, designing her own line of merchandise, and hosting her own talk show.

The talented "domestic arts diva" was born in Jersey City, New Jersey, on August 3, 1941, the second of six children to Martha and Edward Kostyra.
A straight-A student in school, Martha learned gardening from her father and sewing and cooking from her mother. While studying at Barnard College, Martha began modeling and had a lucrative career appearing in several print and television ads for Clairol, Lifebuoy soap, and Chanel fragrances. But it was through her home catering business that Martha Stewart gained her original recognition. Within 10 years she had grown the business into a $1 million enterprise. Catering publishing parties in New York led to a book contract and the release of the bestseller *Martha Stewart's Entertaining*.

In 1990 Stewart launched her magazine *Martha Stewart Living*, and was becoming a familiar guest on shows like *Oprah* and *Larry King Live*. As her popularity grew, so did her business empire. In 1997 she purchased all of the publishing, broadcasting, merchandise, and licensing ventures bearing her name and formed a new company called Martha Stewart Living Omnimedia (MSLO).

Stewart's reputation was tarnished in 2004, when she was convicted of misleading federal investigators looking into insider trading on the stock market. After serving five months in prison, Stewart began rebuilding her reputation and her company, which continues to flourish under her leadership.

explores the use of fresh and seasonal ingredients in cooking. And he adds a gourmet touch to the organic foods philosophy, educating the viewer about foods that are better for the environment and emphasizing the use of top-quality ingredients in healthy everyday cooking.

At his restaurants and in his home, Emeril has lived what he's teaching. A few years earlier, he proudly described in an interview how his then two-and-a-half-year old son had been exposed only to fresh, local foods. "E. J. doesn't know what chicken nuggets are," Emeril said. "He eats fresh chicken soup. He eats lamb steak, broccoli, corn. Where we live, he knows Mikey at the fish market. He knows Leonard at the butcher across the street. He's two and a half years old, he goes in the back, he sees the guys cutting the fish. To me, that's what it's all about."

In another interview, Lagasse recalled how his family had a backyard garden while he was growing up and that he also worked on his uncle's farm in nearby Westport. "Making the connection between food and the people who grow it has always stuck with me," he explained. "Being exposed at an early age to growing and harvesting food from my dad's garden and my Uncle Oliver's farm gave me an appreciation of how farming works and the fresh ingredients that come from that. It's at the root of who I am as a chef."

Planet Green renewed the series in April 2009. In March 2010 Lagasse received a nomination for a Broadcast Media Award in the category Television Special for the *Emeril Green* episode "Emeril's Culinary Adventures: Napa."

CASINO COOKING

Although he was born and raised in the Northeast region of the United States, Emeril did not open a restaurant there until 2009. That May he opened Emeril's Chop House at the Sands Casino Resort Bethlehem. The casino resort was being developed on the site of the former Bethlehem Steel plant in Bethlehem, Pennsylvania.

A few months later, in November, Lagasse added a second restaurant to the Sands Casino Resort. It was his first burger restaurant, called Burgers and More by Emeril. The menu featured prime and grass-fed beef burgers, as well as seafood, turkey, and vegetarian meals.

Lagasse would open a third restaurant at the Pennsylvania casino resort in the summer of 2011. Emeril's Italian Table features rustic Italian-inspired fare such as antipasti, soups and fresh salads, and handmade pastas. The restaurant has an antipasto bar that offers artisan cheeses and cured meats and a wood-burning oven for baking pizzas.

In 2009 Emeril opened another restaurant in The Palazzo Las Vegas Resort Hotel. Lagasse's Stadium featured a sports bar and "entertainment venue"—walls covered with nearly 100 high definition screens for watching most college and professional sporting events. The eatery opened in September with a grand tailgating celebration.

Lagasse's Stadium was Emeril's third venture with The Palazzo and adjoining Venetian Resort-Hotel-Casino. His other two restaurants there were the Delmonico Steakhouse at The Venetian and Table 10 at The Palazzo.

BOOK CONTRACT

Lagasse took on a huge writing assignment when he signed a deal with HarperCollins Publishers to author 10 cookbooks. But he quickly produced two books, both in 2009. In April *Emeril at the Grill: A Cookbook for All Seasons*, was released. It featured recipes for grilled dishes that can be made year round. Within three weeks it had reached No. 8 on the *New York Times* bestseller list in the paperback/advice/how-to category.

The following October saw the publication of *Emeril 20-40-60: Fresh Food Fast*, which provided 140 recipes for quick meals for families. Some could be created within 20 minutes, others in 40 minutes, and still others in 60 minutes or less.

IRON CHEF AMERICA

Lagasse started off the year 2010 in style, with an appearance on what would become one of Food Network's most watched shows of all time. In January he appeared with three other chefs on a special two-hour episode of the network's hit program *Iron Chef America*. He was teamed with Mario Batali in a competition against Bobby Flay and White House executive chef Cristeta Comerford.

The show, which had been taped the previous fall, opened at the White House, in Washington, D.C., where the three chefs met first lady Michelle Obama and Comerford. As in the regular show, the special required them to use a "secret ingredient" in a cooking competition. In this case the secret ingredient was produce from the White House kitchen garden.

The cooking competition between two teams took place at *Iron Chef America*'s Kitchen Stadium in New York City. Each team had one hour to prepare five dishes, which would be judged according to the categories of taste, plating, and originality. The team awarded the highest score would win $25,000 for the charity of its choice.

The dishes prepared by Batali and Lagasse were a scallop, radish, and fennel salad; an oyster and salad trio; sweet potato and cheese ravioli; a quail and turkey duet; and heirloom carrot beignets. Flay and Comerford presented an oyster, fennel, and apple salad; a garden salad with lobster and squid; broccoli clam chowder; a barbeque with pork and a collard green tamale; and a meringue sweet potato tart.

The two teams tied in the taste category, but Flay and Comerford had a slight edge in presentation and originality, thus winning the competition. But the overall winner was the

This billboard promotes the Iron Chef America *"Super Chef Battle," in which Emeril teamed up with Mario Batali to compete against Bobby Flay and White House executive chef Cristeta Comerford. The January 2010 special drew the highest ratings in the Food Network's history.*

Food Network. "Super Chef Battle: An *Iron Chef America* Event" drew 7.6 million viewers, becoming the highest-rated show in the network's history.

NEW ORLEANS COMEBACK

One of the biggest symbols of New Orleans' comeback was the New Orleans Saints participation in the Super Bowl in February 2010. An avid sports fan, Emeril was happy to advise people what to eat at their Super Bowl parties. "If you ask people what the top five foods are for Super Bowl, they'll say chicken wings, salsa, chili, ribs and pizza," he said. "If you ask someone from New Orleans what are your five Super Bowl dishes, they'll tell you gumbo, red beans and rice, jambalaya, roasted pork butt and crawfish."

CNN reported that five years after Katrina, there were 300 more restaurants in the city than had been there before the hurricane. The result of pouring money into refurbishing tourist attractions such as the Convention Center and hotels was a return of the tourism industry.

One of the restaurants that had been in New Orleans before and after Katrina celebrated its 20th year in business that March. Lagasse acknowledged the anniversary of the establishment of his first restaurant, Emeril's, by broadcasting his radio show from the restaurant's dining room.

Cooking with Emeril, a live, weekly call-in show, had debuted the previous November. It aired twice a week on

Emeril provided the voice of Marlon the Gator in the 2009 Disney animated film *The Princess and the Frog*, a fairy tale set in the city of New Orleans.

"Bam!" Emeril continues to deliver the type of high-energy cooking demonstration for which he has become famous.

Martha Stewart Living Radio on SIRIUS XM. For the program Emeril traveled to various places, where he interviewed local chefs and food producers and sampled their food. He also shared his own recipes, culinary tips, and entertaining ideas. Listeners were invited to call in with questions.

Emeril began hosting another new television show in April 2010. The series was the first original programming for the national cable network ION (formerly called PAX). *The Emeril Lagasse Show* was a weekly, prime-time program recorded before a live studio audience in New York with the intent to "capture Emeril's passion for people, entertainment, music, food and celebration." The hour-long variety show launched with a "housewarming party" featuring Martha Stewart and the music of a house band led by jazz saxophonist Dave Koz. The show was to feature various celebrity guests, but it did not receive good reviews. ION cancelled it four months later.

BP OIL SPILL

In mid-2010 the Gulf coast was dealing with another catastrophe. The April 20 explosion of a British Petroleum (BP) offshore oilrig, located in the Gulf of Mexico, caused oil to gush into the waters. As the oil spread toward the Gulf coast shore, areas impacted by the spill were designated as restricted. No seafood could be harvested, which meant most local fisheries and fishermen had to shut down operations. The oil spill was one of the worst environmental disasters in the nation's history, and it had a major financial impact on the Gulf coast.

That summer Emeril, along with other celebrities with roots in the region, filmed a public service announcement. He, along with Sandra Bullock, Dave Matthews, and Peyton Manning, asked that Congress provide the funding necessary to restore the Gulf coast.

Around the same time Lagasse released another cookbook, *Farm to Fork: Cooking Local, Cooking Fresh*. In the book he offered recipes to inspire people to make use of fresh, organic, and locally grown seasonal produce. The cookbook was dedicated to "all the farmers and fishermen (and women) who keep on keepin' on."

When asked in an interview what the dedication meant, Emeril referred to the BP oil spill, saying, "If you look at the Gulf coast fishers, it's easy to understand going beyond the call of duty. They brave the waters as part of their daily lives and have endured really hard times recently—first with hurricanes

The 2010 oil spill in the Gulf of Mexico was one of the worst environmental disasters in U.S. history. It threatened the livelihood of restaurant owners like Emeril, who depend on fresh seafood from the gulf for their establishments. (Top) A small dead fish lies in oil-soaked debris on an Alabama beach. More than 8,000 birds, sea turtles, and marine mammals were found injured or dead in the six months after the spill. (Center) State and federal wildlife officials attempt to catch an oil-covered pelican in Louisiana's Barataria Bay, June 2010. Numerous birds were caught, cleaned, and successfully returned to the wild. (Bottom) Thick oil washed up on many gulf beaches. Thanks to lobbying by Emeril and other celebrities, the government acted quickly enough to protect Louisiana's beaches and coastal wetlands from the worst of the oil.

Katrina and Rita, and now with the oil spill—to keep on providing us with wonderful seafood."

FRESH FOOD FAST

In July 2010 another series starring Emeril launched, this one for the Cooking Channel. *Fresh Food Fast* features Lagasse showing viewers how to select local produce and

Emeril on the set of his Cooking Channel show Fresh Food Fast with Emeril Lagasse.

prepare meals quickly. Half-hour episodes consist of him shopping in fresh food markets and giving cooking demonstrations in the kitchen.

While marketing and filming an episode in New York City, the energetic chef enthused over the popularity of cooking when he told *USA Today*, "The cool thing is that now that people have made this evolution where cooking is cool, people are doing it on weekends, they're doing their own challenges," Lagasse. "It's back to cooking. And it's real cooking."

NEW YORK LIVING

For several years Emeril and his wife Alden have made New York City their home. In 2009 the Lagasses bought a 6,900-square-feet, five-bedroom townhouse in Manhattan and had it renovated.

The home became their primary residence and E. J. and Meril attend school in New York City. Emeril's daughters from his previous marriage, Jessica and Jillian have both married, and Emeril has a grandson.

In February 2009 Emeril received the Lifetime Achievement Award from Food Network's South Beach Wine and Food Festival.

Emeril salutes his audience at the end of a show. The chef's amazing success has enabled him to engage in charitable work that benefits many good causes.

CHAPTER EIGHT

KICKIN' IT
UP A NOTCH

Lagasse devotes around a thousand hours per year traveling to, cooking for, and lending support to fundraisers for various charities. They have included the Susan B. Komen Race for the Cure, the Cystic Fibrosis Foundation, the food rescue organization Table to Table, and the Andre Agassi Foundation for Education.

Emeril has also participated in many fundraisers for Food Bank for New York City, a charitable organization that provides support for food pantries and food kitchens in the city. In April 2010 he was himself honored at the organization's annual "Can-Do Awards Dinner."

EMERIL LAGASSE FOUNDATION

The philanthropic work of Emeril's foundation was part of the reason that Lagasse was given the Can-Do Award. The Foundation raises the bulk of its money at its yearly Carnivale du Vin event, held each November. Over the years it has brought in funds ranging from $1.7 to $2 million per year.

In November 2011 the annual one-night fundraiser became a weekend-long charity gala when a low-cost event called Boudin and Beer was added to the weekend of the traditional Carnivale du Vin. Tickets for the Boudin and Beer fundraiser—a celebration of food, music, and fun—cost just $75 (as opposed to the $1,000 price tag for the Carnivale du Vin).

Hosted by Lagasse, Mario Batali, and Donald Link, the 2011 food and music celebration included city and regional chefs creating their signature boudin and artisanal sausages. Most of the participating chefs were from New Orleans, and included Frank Brigtsen, Susan Spicer, and Paul Prudhomme.

The total funds raised for the Foundation from its inaugural event in 2005 to the 2011 fundraiser is almost $14 million. Other money has come to the Emeril Lagasse Foundation from corporate and individual donations. This has enabled the Foundation to grant funds to many different children's organizations. Since the disasters of Hurricane Katrina and the BP oil spill have struck the Gulf coast particularly hard, most grants have gone to New Orleans charities and Gulf coast area organizations that work to educate children and young adults.

EDIBLE SCHOOLYARD NEW ORLEANS

One of the New Orleans projects funded by the Foundation is the Edible Schoolyard New Orleans (ESY NOLA) program. It provides outdoor classrooms, gardens, fresh foods cafeterias, and teaching kitchens at FirstLine public charter schools in New Orleans.

Founded in 2006, ESY NOLA works to change the way kids eat, learn, and live. Students are involved with growing and harvesting food in the gardens and then in preparing and

The Edible Schoolyard New Orleans at Green Charter School is a teaching garden and kitchen program based on the Edible Schoolyard in Berkeley, California, a program founded by chef and foods activist Alice Waters.

eating meals prepared from that food. Organic gardening and cooking are integrated into the school curriculum, culture, and cafeteria programs in order to encourage kids to choose fresh local ingredients and prepare them in a healthy way.

The Emeril Lagasse Foundation has provided grants to support the ESY NOLA program at Samuel J. Green Charter Elementary School. That money has helped build an outdoor classroom, gardens, and a teaching kitchen and cafeteria at the school.

CAFÉ RECONCILE

Among the first grants made by the Foundation was a $250,000 grant for construction of a culinary learning center at Café Reconcile, a nonprofit youth organization that helps get kids off the streets and into the hospitality industry.

Located in a crime-ridden neighborhood of downtown New Orleans, Café Reconcile is a small restaurant founded in 2000 as a place where at-risk youth could earn money while learning restaurant skills. As of 2011 more than 300 students between the ages of 16 and 25 have gone through the six-week program, obtaining experience working the food service line, waiting tables, and dealing with customers. The experience has helped them get jobs in the New Orleans hospitality industry. The center also provides programs on money skills, drug counseling, and literacy.

The Emeril Lagasse Foundation grant will help Café Reconcile create an institute that provides more advanced culinary training, as well as a place to operate catering services. "Emeril wants to help them take things to the next level," explains Kristen Shannon, the foundation's executive director. "This will help Café Reconcile become even more of a hub for the whole community."

NEW ORLEANS CENTER FOR CREATIVE ARTS (NOCCA)

The Foundation has also become a lead backer for a new program at the New Orleans Center for the Creative Arts (NOCCA). This city high school is known for training aspiring musicians, dancers, and painters. In March 2011 it launched a comprehensive four-year professional training program in culinary arts for high school students.

In March 2011 Lagasse joined NOCCA faculty and staff at a ribbon-cutting ceremony and evening reception to kick off the new culinary arts program and newly constructed teaching kitchen. The Emeril Lagasse Foundation granted more than $500,000 to develop the program's curriculum, in partnership with Johnson and Wales University—Lagasse's alma mater. The first class of students enrolled that fall.

Through his endowed scholarship program, funded by the annual Emeril Lagasse Golf Tournament, Emeril helps four Johnson and Wales culinary arts students pay tuition each year. As of 2011 the tournament had raised approximately $4 million.

"We certainly could have never done what we've done without Emeril," NOCCA's executive director Sally Perry told the *Times-Picayune*. "We had talked about (a culinary arts program) before, but people have talked to NOCCA about a variety of things—architecture, fashion, landscape architecture—and they've never really brought a vision. Emeril brought us a vision about what we could do for young artists with food, and it makes so much sense that if there's going to

EMERIL'S HOMEBASE

Located on St. Charles Avenue in New Orleans, Emeril's Homebase houses Lagasse's corporate office, restaurant operations, test kitchens for cookbook and recipe development and testing, the emerils.com website, product shipping, and a storefront for his signature products. The people who work in the building include culinary writers, test kitchen personnel, accountants, marketing and publicity agents, human resources workers, and salespeople.

Although Homebase employs many types of workers with a wide variety of skills, the office does not accept unsolicited resumes or applications to work there. One of the best ways to try for a job working for Chef Emeril is to apply for a position at one of his restaurants. Workers with excellent culinary skills and eager, positive attitudes do well. Those who show promise as managers are selected for a management development program. They receive hands-on training to prepare them to take on the role of restaurant manager.

be something like that in the country, that it should be in New Orleans."

THE ORIGINALS WITH EMERIL

When not working on philanthropic projects, Lagasse has been busy with television ventures. In May 2011 the Cooking Channel premiered a new series that he hosted. In *The Originals with Emeril*, the chef travels around the United States and showcases historic restaurants that have become icons in their cities.

In the show's first season, aired during primetime, the episodes covered iconic eateries in Atlanta, New York, Los Angeles, Chicago, San Francisco, Boston, Dallas, Miami, and New Orleans. In each city, Emeril visited three historic restaurants and interviewed chefs and customers. "Everybody's doing something new, so I'm doing something old," he said when describing the new show. "I'm going to restaurants around the country that have been in business 50, 75, 100 years. Places that are still in business, and are doing it right."

EMERIL'S TABLE

Another new series hosted by Lagasse debuted in September 2011, this time on the Hallmark Channel. The daily cooking show *Emeril's Table* was produced in association with Martha Stewart Living Omnimedia.

In 2011 *Forbes* estimated that Emeril's media empire, products, and restaurants generate approximately $150 million annually in revenue.

The new program Originals with Emeril *began airing on the Cooking Channel during 2011. (Top) Emeril makes a pizza at Lombardi's Coal Oven Pizza in New York's Little Italy neighborhood with owner John Brescio. Lombardi's, founded in 1905, claims to be the first pizzeria in the United States. (Bottom) Emeril meets with customers at Pink's, a legendary hot dog stand in Hollywood, California, known for its chili dogs.*

The setting for this show is more intimate than that of his boisterous *Emeril Live!* program. In *Emeril's Table* the chef sits down with a group of five people and shares a cooking lesson and recipes chosen especially for that group. The emphasis is more on teaching, which Lagasse says, he did a lot of in running his dining establishments. "I think the biggest thing in the restaurants, and why Emeril's has survived 22 years, is [what] I have done since day one—mentoring," Lagasse told the *Times-Picayune*. "These young culinarians, they want to learn, they want to be taught, they want to be mentored, they want to be lectured." His new show, he says, provides a way for him to teach.

The same month *Emeril's Table* debuted, another Emeril cookbook appeared. *Sizzling Skillets and Other One-Pot Wonders* features

Emeril Lagasse continues to inspire millions of people to enjoy food and cooking.

more than 130 easy recipe ideas for dishes cooked in the cast-iron skillet, casserole, Dutch oven, wok, or slow cooker.

TOP CHEF: TEXAS

Emeril has also taken on a role in reality television. After serving as a guest judge on Bravo network's acclaimed cooking show competition *Top Chef* in 2009, Lagasse was asked to be a regular judge in season nine.

Top Chef: Texas, hosted by Padma Lakshmi, premiered in November 2011 with Emeril as one of the new judges. The competition takes place in the Texas cities of Austin, Dallas, and San Antonio.

AN INNOVATOR AND LEADER

Emeril Lagasse continues to receive acclaim for his work—as a chef, restaurateur, television personality, businessman, author, and philanthropist. In the summer of 2011, at its annual Chefs and Champagne New York Fundraiser, the James Beard Foundation honored Lagasse. Its president praised him for being "an innovator and leader in the food world."

More than a decade after he caught the attention of the nation with his innovative cooking shows, Emeril is still educating, entertaining, and enjoying himself. And he is still finding ways to make the most out of whatever he does—by kickin' it up a notch.

CHAPTER NOTES

p. 7: "There's no smoke and . . ." Bruce Schoenfeld, "Emeril's Empire," *Cigar Aficionado* (October 1, 2005). http://www.cigaraficionado.com/webfeatures/show/id/6192

p. 12: "there's not going to . . ." Kim Severson and Julia Moskin, "Crawfish Etouffee Goes into Exile," *New York Times* (September 6, 2005). http://www.nytimes.com/2005/09/06/business/06restaurant.html?scp=1&sq=&st=nyt

p. 12: "Over the past two . . ." "Emeril Lagasse Dedicated to Rebirth of New Orleans," Emerils.com (September 16, 2005). http://www.emerils.com/newsroom/215/emeril-lagasse-dedicated-to-rebirth-of-new-orleans-3/

p. 13: "The New Orleans restaurant . . ." "Emeril Lagasse Dedicated to Rebirth of New Orleans."

p. 13: "I know this is . . ." Brett Anderson, "Where's Emeril?" *Times-Picayune* (October 15, 2005).

p. 14: "We are very happy . . ." "Emeril Lagasse Announces Dec 05 Reopening Dates of Emeril's and NOLA" Emerils.com (November 2, 2005). http://www.emerils.com/newsroom/125/emeril-lagasse-announces-dec-05-re-opening-dates-of-emerils-restaurant-and-nola-2/

p. 14: "It's sad a city . . ." Gina Edwards, "Emeril Lagasse Lets the Good Times Roll," *Naples (Florida) Daily News* (January 28, 2006). http://www.naplesnews.com/news/2006/jan/28/emeril_lagasse_lets_good_times_roll/

p. 14: "Staffing and housing have . . ." Joyce Sáenz Harris, "Newsroom: *Dallas Morning News*," Emerils.com (October 4, 2006). http://www.emerils.com/newsroom/250/the-dallas-morning-news/

p. 15: "Carnivale du Vin will . . ." "Top Chefs and Vintners to Celebrate New Orleans Spirit in Las Vegas," Emerils.com (October 27, 2005). http://www.emerils.com/newsroom/49/top-chefs-and-vintners-to-celebrate-new-orleans-spirit-in-las-vegas/

p. 16: "His restaurants Emeril's and . . ." Tom Fitzmorris "Commentary: Unique Reinvention Makes Galatoire's Restaurant of the Year," AllBusiness.com (January 8, 2007). http://www.allbusiness.com/north-america/united-states-louisiana/4058770-1.html

p. 16: "In the aftermath of . . ." Fitzmorris, "Commentary."

p. 16: "They were taking potshots . . ." Sam Sifton, "Critic's Notebook: In New Orleans, the Taste of a Comeback, *New York Times* (April 27, 2010). http://www.nytimes.com/2010/04/28/dining/28note.html?pagewanted=all

p. 19: "Portuguese all the way." Rand Richards Cooper, "Essence of

Emeril," *Food and Wine* (November 2000).
http://www.foodandwine.com/articles/essence-of-emeril

p. 20:   "We always had . . ." Linda Richards, "January Interview: Emeril Lagasse," *January Magazine* (November 2000). http://january-magazine.com/profiles/emeril.html

p. 20:   "He wanted to be . . ." Marcia Layton Turner, *Emeril: Inside the Amazing Success of Today's Most Popular Chef* (Hoboken, N.J.: John Wiley and Sons, 2004), p. 12.

p. 21:   "The first thing that . . ." Arthur Greenwald, "Kicking It Up a Notch: An Interview with Star Chef Emeril Lagasse," ZineZone.com (1999). http://www.communitybridge.com/zz/zones/eat/cooking/lagasse/interview1.html

p. 21:   "I'd walk in and . . ." Tim Grenda, "The Accents of Emeril," *Orange Coast* (March 2002), p. 57.

p. 22:   "Her life was food . . ." Kevin P. O'Connor, "Fall River's Ines DeCosta, Who Taught Emeril Lagasse to Cook, Dies at 79," *Herald News* (September 26, 2011). http://www.heraldnews.com/features /x981214642/Fall-Rivers-Ines-DeCosta-who-taught-Emeril-Lagasse-to-cook-dies-at-79

p. 23:   "I didn't have to . . ." Greenwald, "Kicking It Up a Notch."

p. 23:   [N]obody in the early . . ." Schoenfeld, "Emeril's Empire."

p. 23:   "Hey, it's Fall River . . ." Doreen Iudica Vigue, "Kicking It Up a Notch," *Boston Globe* (April 26, 1998).

p. 23:   "I remember sitting . . ." John Grossman, "Recipe for Success," *Cigar Aficionado* (January 1, 1998). http://www.cigaraficionado.com /webfeatures/show/id/Recipe-for-Success_6067

p. 25:   "My mom freaked out . . ." Turner, *Emeril*, p. 16.

p. 26:   "[I]f you think..." "Celeb Chef Stirs Up a Passion for Food," CNN.com (2001). http://www.cnn.com/CNN/Programs/people/shows /lagasse/profile.html.

p. 27:   "Music still is a part . . ." Grenda, "The Accents of Emeril," p. 54.

p. 29:   "I chose Johnson and . . ." Greenwald, "Kicking It Up a Notch."

p. 30:   "Americans weren't supposed to . . ." David Sheff, "Emeril Lagasse," *Playboy*, (February 1999).

p. 30:   "[In] New York . . ." Schoenfeld, "Emeril's Empire."

p. 31:   "You got laughed at . . ." Sheff, "Emeril Lagasse."

p. 31:   "But that was . . ." Sheff, "Emeril Lagasse."

p. 32:   "Food is an equal part," Turner, *Emeril*, p. 19.

p. 33:   "how to work on . . ." Grossman, "Recipe for Success."

p. 33:   "worked me hard." Sheff, "Emeril Lagasse."

p. 34:   "It was his first . . ." "Acadia's Cajuns," *Portland Monthly* (Summer 2010). http://www.portlandmonthly.com/portmag/2010/06/acadias-cajuns/

p. 34:   "He went on . . ." "Acadia's Cajuns," *Portland Monthly*.

p. 36:   "Every week we would . . ." Grossman, "Recipe for Success."

p. 36:   "The enthusiasm, the integrity . . ." Grossman, "Recipe for Success."

p. 40:   "When I first arrived in . . ." Turner, *Emeril*, p. 39.

p. 40:   "Fusion is what made . . ." Sheff, "Emeril Lagasse."

p. 40:   "food whose roots are planted . . ." Emeril Lagasse, *Emeril's New New Orleans Cuisine* (New York: William Morrow, 1993).

p. 41:   "Once Emeril got down . . ." Emeril Lagasse Profile: Celeb Chef Stirs Up a Passion for Food," CNN People in the News (2001). http://www.cnn.com/CNN/Programs/people/shows/lagasse/profile.html

p. 43:   "I guess I feel . . ." Victoria Forrest, "A Conversation with Emeril Lagasse," FabulousFoods.com (Aug 06, 2007). http://www.fabulous-foods.com/articles/21163/a-conversation-with-emeril-lagasse

p. 46:   "trying to bring back . . ." Pamela Parseghian, "The New New Orleans," *Nation's Restaurant News* (February 1, 1993). http://findar-ticles.com/p/articles/mi_m3190/is_n5_v27/ai_13387599/

p. 47:   "quintessential New Orleans chef" "Julia Child: Cajun Cooking with Emeril Lagasse," *Cooking with Master Chefs*, PBS Video, http://video.pbs.org/video/1094273768/

p. 49:   "For the previous four . . ." Schoenfeld, "Emeril's Empire."

p. 49:   "just wanting to . . ." Grenda, "The Accents of Emeril."

p. 50:   "I'd be in the . . ." Grossman, "Recipe for Success."

p. 50:   "From the beginning, Emeril . . ." Emeril Lagasse, Marcel Bienvenu, and Felicia Willett, *Emeril's TV Dinners: Kickin' It Up a Notch with Recipes from Emeril Live and Essence of Emeril* (New York: William Morrow, 1998).

p. 50:   "It was like, BAM! to wake . . ." Edwards, "Emeril Lagasse Lets the Good Times Roll."

p. 53:   "It's a very demanding . . ." Gary James, "Emeril Lagasse Interview," FamousInterview.com (1996). http://www.famousinterview.ca/inter-views/emeril_lagasse.htm

p. 53:   "I think that . . ." Turner, Emeril, p. 121.

p. 53:   "I'm just not into . . ." Grenda, "The Accents of Emeril," p. 56.

p. 54:   "A lot of professional foodies . . ." Amanda Hesser, "Under the Toque; 'Here's Emeril!' Where's the Chef?" *New York Times* (November 4, 1998).

p. 54:   "one of the tube's most . . ." Michelle Green, "Season's Eatings," *People* (December 22, 1997). http://www.people.com/people/archive/article/0,,20124106,00.html

p. 54:   "The 28 million viewers . . ." Green, "Season's Eatings."

p. 55:   "I can impart my . . ." Sheff, "Emeril Lagasse."

p. 56:   "We're going to bring back . . ." Grossman, "Recipe for Success."

p. 60:   "the cornerstone of the . . ." "Food Network and Emeril Lagasse Sign Five-Year, Multi-Million Dollar Deal," Scripps: Press Room (May 7, 2003). http://pressreleases.scripps.com/release/618

p. 61:   "Whatever it is, I'm . . ." Schoenfeld, "Emeril's Empire."

p. 64:   "They won't lose . . ." Karen Grigsby Bates, "'Emeril's Delmonico': A Classic Take on Creole," National Public Radio (October 19, 2005). http://www.npr.org/templates/story/story.php?storyId=4965420

p. 66:   "So many chefs were . . ." Brett Anderson, "Boudin and Beer Party
           Brings Locals to the Table for Emeril's Foundation," *Times-Picayune*
           (November 10, 2011). http://www.nola.com/dining/index.ssf/2011
           /11/boudin_beer_party_brings_local.html

p. 67:   "You can't buy this . . ." Sifton, "Critic's Notebook: In New Orleans,
           the Taste of a Comeback."

p. 68:   "We spent easily . . ." Mary Foster, Associated Press, "With Martha's
           Help Emeril Going Strong 20 Years On," *Bloomberg Businessweek*
           (April 19, 2010). http://www.businessweek.com/ap/financialnews
           /D9F68DKG0.htm

p. 70:   "It's an absolute honor . . ." National Aeronautics and Space
           Administration, "Station Crew 'Kicks it Up a Notch' with Chef
           Emeril Lagasse," August 10, 2006. http://www.nasa.gov/mission_pages
           /station/behindscenes/emeril_ISS_food.html

p. 70:   "We sampled the food . . ." National Aeronautics and Space
           Administration, "Station Crew 'Kicks it Up a Notch' with Chef
           Emeril Lagasse."

p. 71:   "From a food perspective . . ." Harris, "Newsroom: Dallas Morning
           News."

p. 72:   "I know we're all . . ." Harris, "Newsroom: Dallas Morning News."

p. 72:   "I receive offers every . . ." "Island View and Emeril LaGasse Unveil
           Plans for Gulfport Restaurant," Emerils.com (November 20, 2006).
           http://www.emerils.com/newsroom/80/island-view-emeril-lagasse-
           unveil-plans-for-gulfport-restaurant/#more-80

p. 72:   "comfort food, gone . . ." Rachel M. Sugay, "Restaurant Review:
           Table 10," *Today in Las Vegas Magazine* (February 2010).
           http://todayinlv.com/rest_rvws/Table%2010%20-%20Palazzo.html

p. 73:   "I am deeply appreciative . . ." "Food Network Cancels 'Emeril
           Live,'" EW.com, (November 27, 2007). http://www.ew.com/ew/arti-
           cle/0,,20162691,00.html

p. 75:   "We have been able . . ." "Stewart's Company Acquires Emeril
           Assets," UPI.com (February 19, 2008).
           http://www.upi.com/Entertainment_News/2008/02/19/Stewarts-com-
           pany-acquires-Emeril-assets/UPI-81731203462680/#ixzz1gVN6vk5y

p. 75:   "His remarkable talents . . ." Foster, "With Martha's Help Emeril
           Going Strong 20 Years On."

p. 76:   "She showed up at . . ." Foster, "With Martha's Help Emeril Going
           Strong 20 Years On."

p. 78:   "E. J. doesn't know . . ." Schoenfeld, "Emeril's Empire."

p. 78:   "Making the connection . . ." Nancy Rutman, "The Fresh Chef,"
           Organic Gardening, v. 57 no. 5 (August/September 2010), p. 52.

p. 82:   "If you ask people . . ." Jacquelynn D. Powers, "Who Dat? Exclusive
           Emeril Lagasse Interview," *Miami New Times* (February 5, 2010).
           http://blogs.miaminewtimes.com/shortorder/2010/02/who_dat_exclu-
           sive_emeril_lagas.php

p. 83:   "capture Emeril's passion . . ." "Emeril Gets New Show on ION,"

UPI.com, (January 20, 2010). http://www.upi.com/Entertainment_
News/TV/2010/01/20/Emeril-gets-new-show-on-ION/UPI-
64791264021241/#ixzz1gVNPg31l

p. 84:   "If you look at . . ." Rutman, "The Fresh Chef."

p. 87:   "The cool thing is . . ." Andrea Mandell, "Emeril Gets a 'Fresh' Start
on Food Show," *USA Today* (July 2, 2010). http://www.usatoday.com
/printedition/life/20100702/emeril02_cv.art.htm

p. 92:   "Emeril wants to help . . ." Theodore P. Mahne, "Keeping Body and
Soul Together," *Times-Picayune* (November 10, 2006).

p. 93:   "We certainly could have never . . ." Anderson, "Boudin and Beer
Party Brings Locals to the Table for Emeril's Foundation."

p. 94:   "Everybody's doing something . . ." J. M. Hirsch and Holly Ramer,
"Emeril's New Show to Delve into Some Historic Restaurants,"
Arlington Heights (IL) Daily Herald (March 9, 2011), Lifestyle: p. 2.

p. 96:   "I think the biggest . . ." Dave Walker, "For 'Emeril's Table,' New
Orleans Superstar Chef Downsizes," *Times-Picayune* (September 26,
2011). http://www.nola.com/tv/index.ssf/2011/09/for_emerils_table
_new_orleans.html

p. 97:   "an innovator and leader . . ." Press Release "James Beard
Foundation to "Kick It Up a Notch" at Annual Chefs and
Champagne New York Fundraiser and Tasting Gala Honoring Emeril
Lagasse," (February 2, 2011).

CHRONOLOGY

1959: Emeril John Lagasse III is born on October 15, 1959, in Fall River, Massachusetts.

1969: At age 10, Emeril gets his first job, as a dishwasher at Moonlight Bakery; by age 12, he is working there on the night shift.

1983: Accepts a job as executive chef at Commander's Palace, in New Orleans.

1990: Emeril's Restaurant, Lagasse's first dining establishment, opens in New Orleans.

1992: Opens his second restaurant, NOLA.

1993: *Emeril' s New New Orleans Cooking* is published; the Food Network hires Lagasse to host the television program *How to Boil Water*.

1994: Lagasse's first hit TV show, *The Essence of Emeril*, premieres on the Food Network in November.

1995: Opens his third restaurant, Emeril's New Orleans Fish House, in Las Vegas.

1997: In January *Emeril Live!* debuts on the Food Network.

1998: Lagasse takes a position with *Good Morning America* as a food correspondent; opens his third New Orleans restaurant, Emeril's Delmonico.

1999: Introduces Emerilware All-Clad cookware.

2000: Introduces Emeril food products: marinades, seasonings, salad dressings, pasta sauces, and his spice blend "Essence."

2001: Stars in an NBC half-hour sitcom, *Emeril*, which fails quickly.

2002: In September the Emeril Lagasse Foundation is founded; *There's a Chef in My Soup*, Emeril's first cookbook for kids, is published.

2003: Opens three new restaurants, Emeril's Miami Beach, Emeril's Atlanta, and Emeril's Tchoup Chop.

2005: In May Emeril tapes his 1,500th show for the Food Network; in August Hurricane Katrina hits the Gulf coast, forcing Lagasse to shut down his New Orleans restaurants. In December, Emeril's and NOLA reopen.

2006: In August Emeril becomes the first celebrity chef to create meals for NASA astronauts and have them served while in space; in October Emeril's Delmonico reopens in New Orleans.

2008: Martha Stewart Living Omnimedia buys the rights to Emeril Lagasse's cookbooks, television shows, and kitchen products; Lagasse launches a new series on Planet Green network, *Emeril Green*.

2009: A call-in show called *Cooking with Emeril* launches on SIRIUS radio in November.

2010: Lagasse debuts new shows: *The Emeril Lagasse Show* (April to July on ION) and *Fresh Food Fast* (July premiere on the Cooking Channel).

2011: In May Lagasse begins hosting *The Originals with Emeril* on the Cooking Channel; in September *Emeril's Table* launches on the Hallmark Channel.

GLOSSARY

AMBIENCE—the character and atmosphere of a place.

BAYOU—a marshy outlet of a lake or river.

BEIGNET—a square-shaped fried dough sprinkled with confectioners' sugar.

CAJUN—a southern Louisiana style of cooking based on the cuisine of French-speaking or Acadian immigrants; often referred to as rustic cuisine.

CREOLE—a Louisiana style of cooking influenced by French, Native American, and African cultures.

CUISINE—a style or method of cooking.

CULINARY—of or for cooking.

DOYENNE—a woman who is considered the most respected or prominent person in her profession or field of expertise.

ETOUFFEE—a simmered roux-based gravy or sauce served over rice.

FUSION—food or cooking that combines elements of diverse cuisines.

GREEN—connected with or supporting protection of the environment.

HOSPITALITY INDUSTRY—the fields of the service industry related to housing or entertaining people—included are restaurant and hotel industries.

JAMBALAYA—a spicy dish made with rice, tomato, and seafood or meat.

ORGANIC—food produced without the use of chemical fertilizers, pesticides, or other artificial agents.

PALATE—a person's appreciation of taste and flavor.

RESTAURATEUR—a person who owns and manages a restaurant.

ROUX—from French, a base for dishes made from flour and oil or butter.

SHELLFISH—a mollusk (such as oyster) or crustacean (such as crab, shrimp, or crayfish).

FURTHER READING

Lagasse, Emeril. *Emeril 20-40-60: Fresh Food Fast*. New York: HarperStudio, 2009.

———. *Farm to Fork: Cooking Local, Cooking Fresh*. New York: HarperCollins, 2010.

———. *Louisiana Real and Rustic*. New York: William Morrow Cookbooks, 2009.

———. *There's a Chef in My Soup! Recipes for the Kid in Everyone*. New York: HarperCollins, 2005.

Turner, Marcia Layton. *Emeril! Inside the Amazing Success of Today's Most Popular Chef*. Hoboken, N.J.: John Wiley and Sons, 2004.

INTERNET RESOURCES

HTTP://WWW.EMERILS.COM/

The official website of Emeril Lagasse features links to his recipes, restaurants, and biography, as well as to a cooking blog, archived news stories, and a shopping site for Emeril brand products and cookbooks.

HTTP://EMERIL.ORG/

The official website of the Emeril Lagasse Foundation provides news and updates on projects funded by the charity organization.

HTTP://WWW.NEWORLEANSONLINE.COM/NEWORLEANS/
CUISINE/CHEFS/

The official tourism site of the City of New Orleans features information on the city's celebrity chefs, including Lagasse, and their restaurants.

HTTP://PLANETGREEN.DISCOVERY.COM/TV/EMERIL-GREEN/

This Planet Green website links to descriptions of various Emeril Green episodes and provides additional information on that show's topic, including tips and recipes.

HTTP://WWW.FOODNETWORK.COM/EMERIL-LIVE/INDEX.HTML

The Food Network webpage on "Emeril Lagasse on the Cooking Channel" features links to a biography and recipes from the show.

Numbers in **bold italics** refer to captions.

SAWYER ALBRIGHT is a freelance writer who lives near Philadelphia. She holds an EdM in instructional technologies from Temple University. Her free time is devoted to cooking, photography, travel, volunteerism, and her pet cats.

921 Lag
1/13